I0024413

Harry John Wilmont-Buxton

The Lord's Song

Plain Sermons on Hymns

Harry John Wilmont-Buxton

The Lord's Song
Plain Sermons on Hymns

ISBN/EAN: 9783744745277

Printed in Europe, USA, Canada, Australia, Japan

Cover: Foto ©Thomas Meinert / pixelio.de

More available books at **www.hansebooks.com**

The Lord's Song:

PLAIN SERMONS ON HYMNS.

———•———

BY THE

REV. H. J. WILMOT BUXTON, M.A.,

VICAR OF S. GILES-IN-THE-WOOD, NORTH DEVON.

———————

London:

W. SKEFFINGTON & SON, 163, PICCADILLY, W.

—

1880

To

THE REV HENRY J. STEPHENS, B.A.,

VICAR OF WORSTHORNE, LANCASHIRE,

MY FRIEND, AND FELLOW-WORKER IN MANY HAPPY MISSIONS,

THESE SERMONS ARE DEDICATED.

Volumes of Sermons by the Rev. H. J. WILMOT BUXTON.

MISSION SERMONS FOR A YEAR, including Sixty-eight Short Plain Sermons for EVERY SUNDAY; a few SAINTS' DAYS, HARVEST, MISSIONS, FUNERAL, DEDICATION FESTIVAL, &c. Price 7/6, by post 8/2.

"In this volume the same beauty and vigour of language, happiness of metaphor, and strikingness of application are apparent on a larger scale, as in his Children's Sermons. The village congregation is, indeed, exceptionally favoured in its possession of so powerful a preacher."
—*Church Review.*

"We find the idea so well carried out that we cannot but hope that the volume will be widely used. There is something so definite, striking, and even piquant in every sermon, that they cannot fail to be serviceable."
—*Church Quarterly.*

MISSION SERMONS, FIRST SERIES, containing Twenty Plain Sermons. 3/-, by post 3/2. (*This volume is at present out of print.*)

MISSION SERMONS, SECOND SERIES. Thirty Plain Sermons. Besides many on general and miscellaneous subjects, the volume also includes Sermons for ADVENT, CHRISTMAS, LENT, EASTER, TRINITY, HARVEST FESTIVAL, AUTUMN, &c. Third Edition. Cloth, price 4/6, by post 4/9.

SHORT SERMONS FOR CHILDREN, including a few for Young Domestic Servants. A series of Twenty-three. Price 3/6, by post 3/8.

"Very earnest and powerful, and full of evidence of the wide sympathies and cultivated taste of their author. In style they are almost faultless ; simple words, short sentences, straightforward constructions—all that sermon style should be. In short, whilst they are most unpretending, they are sermons of a very high mark indeed, and we would commend them to the younger men among the clergy as models for their own pulpit addresses."—*Literary Churchman.*

"Short and telling sentences, full of illustration and anecdote, with the charm of poetry about them, they are altogether well suited to catch the attention of their hearers."—*Church Times.*

Contents.

" Lead, kindly Light, amid the encircling gloom,
　　Lead Thou me on ;
The night is dark, and I am far from home,
　　Lead Thou me on.
Keep Thou my feet ; I do not care to see
The distant scene ; one step enough for me.

" I was not ever thus, nor prayed that Thou
　　Should'st lead me on ;
I loved to choose and see my path ; but now
　　Lead Thou me on.
I loved the garish day, and spite of fears,
Pride ruled my will ; remember not past years.

" So long Thy power hath blest me, sure it still
　　Will lead me on
O'er moor and fen, o'er crag and torrent, till
　　The night is gone.
And with the morn those angel faces smile,
Which I have loved long since, and lost awhile."

SERMON I.

The Guiding Light.

(ADVENT.)

PSALM LXXVIII. 14.

" In the day time also He led them with a cloud, and all the night with a light of fire."

WHY do we sing hymns? Perhaps it never occurred to you to ask that question, or possibly if you did ask it, you got a wrong answer. Some persons will tell you that they sing hymns because they like the tune, or because they know the words, or because they are fond of hearing their own voice. Yet these are all wrong reasons. I can tell you a story about this. Once there was a little company of monks, who lived in a rude and lonely monastery, in a wild country. Daily they sang the praises of God, but their singing was rude and harsh. One day a stranger came and stayed with them, and the stranger had a very beautiful voice. He soon took the management of the choir into his own hands, he told the monks how rude and coarse was their singing, and he bid them listen to his way of chanting the service. And so

in time there was scarcely any other voice heard in the
choir except that of the stranger. One night the Abbot
saw a vision in which he thought an angel from heaven
appeared, and asked him why they never heard now in
heaven the beautiful praises which used to rise from the
lonely cloister. The Abbot in astonishment explained
that their singing had greatly improved of late. But the
angel answered that not one of the stranger's tuneful
notes had got as far as heaven, since there they heard
only the voice of praise, not of pride and self-righteous-
ness. Some one says very truly that many put hymns of
praise into their mouth to glorify themselves instead of
God. The reason why we should sing hymns is to praise
and honour that God who giveth all. As He gives us
music, and poetry, and voices, so we should consecrate
these gifts to Him. We should forget ourselves, and
think only of Him " who is worthy to be praised." And
not only in Church should we do this, a Christian's
whole life should be a consecrated life, a life of praise.
The world of nature teaches us this, where God has taught

> " The ballad-singers and the Troubadours,
> The street-musicians of the Heavenly city,
> The birds, who make sweet music for us all,
> In our dark hours, as David did for Saul.
> The thrush that carols at the dawn of day,
> From the green steeples of the piny wood,
> Linnet and meadow-lark, and all the throng
> That dwell in nests, and have the gift of song."

" Whether therefore ye eat, or drink, or whatsoever ye do, do all to the glory of God." Our work should be such that we may praise God by it ; our joys should lift us to God in thanksgiving ; our sorrows, instead of crushing us, should lift us up, so that we may say " out of my stony griefs Bethel I'll raise." Thus our whole life should be, so to speak, a hymn of praise, an endless hallelujah.

But there is another reason for singing hymns. They have a lesson for us. There is a sermon in a hymn, as well as in the lesson, or gospel, or epistle for the day. Let us try, by God's help, to bring out some of the teaching of our favourite hymns, that what we sing with our lips, we may believe in our hearts, that we may in a word, " sing praises with understanding." Let us look at the hymn which we have just sung, " Lead, kindly Light." Among the many thoughts which this solemn Advent season brings to us, there is one which the hymn suggests, our need of a guiding light through the darkness of this world. How dark and miserable this earth would be if Jesus Christ had not come to be the Light of the World. How dark our hours of sorrow would be without the light of Christ's sympathy to cheer us ! How black and uncertain our path would be without the light of Christ's Gospel to lead us ! Some time ago I was conducting a Mission in the Black Country, and I went with my brother missioner to hold services in several coalpits. It was a wonderful feeling to find oneself two

hundred yards down in the earth, with the black galleries
of the pit dimly lighted by candles stuck in their clay
sockets ; and it was still more wonderful when we began
to sing a hymn, and the well-known words,

> " Jesu, lover of my soul,
> Let me to Thy bosom fly,"

sounded, perhaps for the first time since the earth was
made, through that strange place. Then followed an
address, listened to with the greatest attention by grimy,
half-clad colliers; the only interruption coming from a
restless pony in his rocky stable, or from a deep *amen*
which one of the listeners uttered as the words went home
to his heart. When the service was over, I explored the
pit, and examined the different workings, and there I
learnt three things which you will do well to learn also.
First, I learnt that I must stoop my head if I wished to
go along the galleries of the pit. And there is a lesson
for us all ; we must stoop our heads, we must be humble,
if we are to pass through this life to life eternal.
Although the gate of Heaven is so high, it is not high
enough for us to enter except on bended knee, and with
bowed head. How shall we best prepare ourselves this
Advent to meet our Lord when He comes again in
glory ? By learning to be humble, even as He tells us,
" learn of Me, for I am meek and lowly." Next, they gave

me a candle in a lump of clay to carry, and as I walked
with bowed head and careful steps, my candle went out.
Now if I had been alone in that strange place I should
have been lost : it was perfectly dark all round me, the
walking was very dangerous, and there were galleries to
the right hand and left, which led to distant parts of the
pit. But I was not alone; I had a guide who went
before me, carrying a light, to show me the way. Then
I learnt that we must have a light in ourselves, and also
a guide to lead us through the darkness of this world, to
the bright day of Paradise. The light in ourselves is the
Holy Spirit, of whom holy David says, "Thou wilt light
my candle." The guide is the light of Christ's example
as given in the Bible, of which it is written, "Thy Word
is a lamp unto my feet, and a light unto my path."

Two words of advice were given me in the coal-pit,
they were "take care of your light," and "follow your
guide." "Take care of your light;" the Holy Spirit was
given to us in Baptism; in Confirmation, and in the
Sacraments, and the various means of grace, that Holy
Spirit is renewed in us, like oil in a lamp. Are we taking
good heed to "let our light so shine before men that
they may see our good works, and glorify our Father
which is in Heaven?" "Follow your guide." Jesus
saith unto us "follow thou Me." If I had chosen my
own way in that dark coal-mine I should soon have lost
myself, or stumbled and fallen. So there are many

people in the world who are like men in a coal-pit whose
light is gone out, and who foolishly choose their own
path, instead of following a guide. There may be some
such wanderers here. May God bring them to say with
truth —

> " I loved to choose and see my path ; but now
> Lead Thou me on."

In the darkness of the coal-pit I could only see a few
yards before me. So it is with us all in life. We may
not see far away into the future ; we have *to-day's* work,
to-day's duty, *to-day's* journey to accomplish, *to-day* the
manna will fall, since God gives us our *daily bread.*
" The morrow will take thought for the things of itself."

> " Keep Thou my feet ; I do not care to see
> The distant scene; one step enough for me."

There are many so-called Christians who fancy they
are walking in the light, but who are really groping in
darkness. These have not learnt what it is to be a
Christian. They have not learnt to be humble, to deny
themselves, to give up self for Christ. Their light is
gone out. Let such people learn these simple lessons.
Let them go in prayer to Jesus, the Light of the World,
He will light their candle. " Awake thou that sleepest,
and arise from the dead, and Christ shall give thee light."

Then with bowed head, and carefully guarded light, go forth on thy pilgrimage,

> " Through terrestrial darkness,
> To celestial day,"

following in the steps of Thy guide, even the steps of Christ's most holy life, praying ever—

> " Lead, kindly Light, amid the encircling gloom,
> Lead Thou me on."

" Guide me, O Thou great Redeemer,
  Pilgrim through this barren land ;
  I am weak, but Thou art mighty,
  Hold me with Thy powerful hand ;
          Bread of Heaven,
  Feed me now and evermore.

" Open now the crystal fountain,
  Whence the healing streams do flow :
  Let the fiery, cloudy pillar,
  Lead me all my journey through ;
          Strong Deliverer,
  Be Thou still my Strength and Shield.

" When I tread the verge of Jordan,
  Bid my anxious fears subside :
  Death of death, and hell's Destruction,
  Land me safe on Canaan's side ;
          Songs of praises,
  I will ever give to Thee."

SERMON II.

The Long Journey.

(ADVENT.)

DEUTERONOMY III. 25.

" I pray thee, let me go over, that I may see the good land that is beyond Jordan."

THIS was the prayer of the old man Moses when weary and worn out with his long life's work. For years he had led the people of Israel, and had suffered their manners in the wilderness. Now his work was done, and he longed for rest, and for a sight of that land towards which he had journeyed so long. His eyes, tired of the desert sand, yearned for the green pastures, and his aching limbs for the rest that remained in the good land beyond Jordan. And yet his prayer was refused. The old sin of long ago was remembered, and Moses was not permitted to enter the promised land. Brave, patient, faithful though he had been, his prayer was refused. God rewarded him indeed by taking him to the better land of Paradise, but the one desire of his long life was not satisfied. We learn from this first of all that one sin

may shut us out of Heaven. Moses had committed a
sin long ago; since then he had done God good service,
yet that sin was not forgotten, it shut him out of the
promised land. Sin always brings its own punishment, at
some time or other, and in some way or another. Some
sins, like some seeds, grow up and bear their bitter fruit
very quickly. Others lie hid for a long time, but they
bear fruit. Learn next, that doing good does not atone
for a past sin. How much good Moses had done, yet
his old sin shut him out from the good land. "All our
obediences," says an old writer of the Church, "cannot
blot out one sin against God." How vain for us to hope
to make amends to God for our former trespasses by our
better behaviour, when Moses had this one sin laid to his
charge after so many proofs of fidelity. When we have
forgotten our sins, God remembers them, and though not
in anger, yet He calls for our arrears. If Moses died the
first death for one fault, how shall they "escape the
second death for sinning always?" Do not think that
the old sins of your past lives are of no importance
because you may have been living decent lives of late.
I tell you we shall not enter into the good land unless
our sins be forgiven us. All our good works cannot wipe
out the old score. True repentance alone can bring us
pardon, through the mediation of Jesus Christ, the
Saviour from all sin.

"I pray thee, let me go over that I may see the good

land that is beyond Jordan." That was the heart's desire of Israel of old, and it is the prayer of us, God's Israel, to-day. Some of us, who have wandered these many years in the wilderness, long very eagerly for that " rest which remaineth for the people of God," and for repose " in that still country where the mystery of this strange life is solved, and the most feverish heart lays down its burden at last." Many a one is tempted some-times, when the sorrow is *very* sharp, and the road very rough, to cry with David, " Oh! that I had wings like a dove, for then would I flee away and be at rest." Many a one, whose earthly work is not yet finished, is tempted sometimes to say, " I pray thee, let me go over, that I may see the good land that is beyond Jordan." But we must remember the journey. Israel had to take a long journey before they entered the Promised Land, and many never entered it at all because of their sins. So it is with us. There is a long journey for us, and our prayer should be,

> " Guide me, O Thou great Redeemer,
> Pilgrim through this barren land;
> I am weak, but Thou art Mighty,
> Hold me with Thy powerful hand.
> Bread of Heaven,
> Feed me now and evermore."

Look at the first step in Israel's journey. They escaped from Pharaoh and the taskmasters of Egypt, and passed through the Red Sea. Pharaoh and his host pursuing them were buried in the Sea. Now look at our own journey. We are born into a world of sin, a world like Egypt, with its hard taskmasters, the Flesh and the Devil. The sin of Adam, our birth sin, and the curse for sin, pursue after us to destroy us. But in Baptism we pass through the Red Sea of Christ's Blood, and our birth sin, and the curse for sin, are buried there like Pharaoh. Our old man, our old sinful nature, as Adam's descendants, is buried with Christ in Baptism, that the new man may be raised up in us. Now look at the second step in the journey. Did Israel find themselves in perfect safety after they had passed through the Red Sea? No, they found themselves in the wilderness, in a place full of enemies. Their old enemies were gone, but new foes awaited them. So it is with us. After Baptism we begin our life in the wilderness. The old sin of Adam is forgiven us, but new sins and temptations await us in the world. Yes, this world is for many reasons a wilderness. We are all in the world as strangers and pilgrims, and some of us live quite alone, like those who journey through the desert. Even those of us who have many friends see them grow fewer as the years roll by. Where are those whom we knew in youth and childhood? Gone over to the greater number, to the more thickly populated world beyond. It has been truly said, "the years darken round us among new men, strange faces, other minds." Again, this life is like a wilderness because it is often very hard to find food in it. I do not mean bodily food, though that is scarce enough to many, but food for the soul. A Christian cannot nourish his soul on this world's food, any more than the foolish king of yore could satisfy his hunger when he had prayed that all that he touched might be changed into gold. There are plenty of people who are living for this life only, who are trying to feed on this world's food, and they starve. One lives for pleasure, and at last he ceases to have the power to enjoy ; another lives for work, and it becomes an irksome slavery. Another lives for money, and he sees it melt away, or he has to leave it to another. Israel would have perished in the wilderness if God had not sent them Bread from Heaven. So we shall all likewise perish unless we derive our spiritual food from God. If we live without God, without prayer, without religion, we must starve, for we shall be without that peace which the world *cannot* give. Above all, we need to pray here in the wilderness,

> " Bread of Heaven,
> Feed me now and evermore ;"

for the journey to the good land beyond Jordan will be too great for us, unless we feed on the true Bread which came down from Heaven, the Body and Blood of Jesus Christ.

Again, we read of Israel in the wilderness, that "hungry

and thirsty their soul fainted within them." So with us, we thirst for that which the wilderness cannot give us. There is water in the world to quench bodily thirst, "but whoso drinketh of this water shall thirst again." Jesus alone can give us " of the Water of life freely." When sin and sorrow lie heavy upon us, when we are forced to say, "I am weary of crying, my throat is dry," Jesus alone can give us that refreshment which we need, "the good news from a far country," which is "as cold water to a thirsty soul."

> "Open now the crystal Fountain,
> Whence the healing streams do flow."

We know also that the wilderness was full of dangers and enemies for Israel of old, so is our life to-day. Thorns beset our path, and choke the good seed. Cares and troubles vex us like the burning sand; often this world becomes " a great and terrible wilderness, wherein are fiery serpents and scorpions." Evil thoughts, fiery lusts, and savage tempers, like serpents, attack us. Bad companions lead us astray, of whom we may say, " the poison of asps is under their lips." Israel, we know, " wandered out of the way," because the wilderness had no clearly defined path for them to travel in. So in the world there are many paths carved out by man's strength, or pride, or selfishness, but none of these lead to the good land beyond Jordan. One will say to us, " Never mind the road to Heaven, enjoy what this earth can give you." Another will whisper, " Work hard, do your best, that is the road to Heaven ;" another will say, "Go on your own way, all will come right at last." Not so, brethren. In Australia it is a common thing to find a man lost and dead in the bush within call of his own home. So in the world many wander out of the path and perish with Heaven before them, because they have lost their way. Jesus alone can show us the Way. He says, " I am the Way, the Truth, and the Life. No man cometh to the Father but by Me."

> " Let the fiery, cloudy pillar,
> Lead me all my journey through;
> Strong Deliverer,
> Be Thou still my Strength and Shield."

Seeing, then, that this world is like a wilderness, where we are strangers and pilgrims ; which cannot satisfy the hungry soul with goodness, nor the parched soul with living water ; where enemies beset us, and which can give us no path to Heaven, surely we need something better than this world to live for, to look for, to work for. The thought of the good land beyond Jordan cheered Israel in their wanderings ; the thought of a still better country should cheer us. When the path of duty seems very hard, when innumerable sorrows have gone even over our soul, when we see the wilderness marked with the

B

graves of our dead, our dead friends, our dead hopes,
our dead joys; when old age, or sickness, or sorrow have
bowed down our bodies, and our weary limbs ache so, that
we are forced to echo the cry of a weary one who said,
"at times I feel the want to die, as the wakeful feel the
want to sleep;" then, at such times as these, there comes
to cheer us the thought of the good land beyond Jordan,
and our prayer goes up to God, "I pray Thee, let me go
over, that I may see the good land."

> "When I tread the verge of Jordan,
>   Bid my anxious fears subside;
>   Death of death, and hell's destruction,
>   Land me safe on Canaan's side;"

But remember, dear fellow pilgrims, we may not hope
to enter into our rest till our *work* is done and our
journey finished.

> "Does the road wind up-hill all the way?
>   Yes; to the very end.
>   Will the day's journey take the whole long day?
>   From morn to night, my friend."

Wishing for Paradise will not take us there. For us all
there is a work to be done, and a given time to do it in.
A quaint old writer tells us that "God sends his servants
to bed when they have done their work." Our journey
through this world must be one of watching, of fighting,
of praying, and of waiting, and when that is over our

Master will give His beloved sleep. When the American saint and hero " Stonewall " Jackson was dying, he said, " let us cross over the river, and rest under the shade of the trees ;" so may we one day hope to cross the river of death, and to see the good land that is beyond Jordan, and to rest under the shadow of the Tree of Life, " whose leaves are for the healing of the nations."

"Christian, dost thou see them,
On the holy ground,
How the troops of Midian
Prowl and prowl around ?
Christian, up and smite them,
Counting gain but loss ;
Smite them by the merit
Of the holy Cross.

"Christian, dost thou feel them,
How they work within,
Striving, tempting, luring,
Goading into sin ?
Christian, never tremble,
Never be down-cast ;
Smite them by the virtue
Of the Lenten fast.

"Christian, dost thou hear them,
How they speak thee fair ?
'Always fast and vigil ?
Always watch and prayer ?'
Christian, answer boldly,
'While I breathe I pray :'
Peace shall follow battle,
Night shall end in day.

"Well I know thy trouble,
O my servant true ;
Thou art very weary,
I was weary too ;
But that toil shall make thee
Some day all Mine own,
And the end of sorrow
Shall be near My throne."

SERMON III.

The Warfare.

(Lent.)

1 PETER V. 9.
" Whom resist, steadfast in the faith."

THE Hymn brings before us a picture of the Christian life as being a warfare, a battle with sin. Every Christian man has a war to wage with his spiritual foes, " for we wrestle not against flesh and blood, but against principalities, against powers, against spiritual wickedness in high places."

> " Christian, dost thou see them,
> On the holy ground,
> How the troops of Midian
> Prowl and prowl around ?"

Yes, on the holy ground; for as Midian of old was permitted to fight against God's Israel, so the devil and his angels attack us on the holiest of ground. As Satan came to Jesus when praying and fasting, so he comes to us within the closet of secret prayer, into the Religious house, to the Church and the Altar itself. You remember

how on a day when the sons of God presented themselves before Him, " Satan came also." So now he
and his angels come *everywhere*, tempting into sin. There
is never a service held in Church where Satan does not
come also ; there is never a Bible opened, nor a prayer
uttered, but Satan comes also, trying to pluck away the
good seed, striving to lead our thoughts astray. When
people kneel in Church, and begin to say the Confession,
"we have erred and strayed from Thy ways like lost
sheep," often their thoughts begin to wander, their sin is
forgotten, and left unconfessed. It is because Satan has
come also, and has led their minds away from their sins,
lest they should confess them and find pardon. Presently
the eyes of some begin to stray, they see a neighbour's
face, or mark a late arrival in Church, and the Prayer
Book is straightway forgotten ; the thread of the Service
lost ; Satan has come also, and led those eyes astray, lest
the people should see with their eyes, and believe in their
hearts and *be saved*. Presently, when the Sermon is
preached, the eyes of some grow heavy with sleep, and
the words of warning and of love fall unheeded. Satan
has come also, and has sent those people to sleep lest
they should be awakened to their true state, and repent
and *be saved*. Or perhaps there are some who are quite
awake, who hear every word of the sermon, and who
criticise it, and find fault with it, and are offended at it.
Again Satan has come also, and has put those proud and

rebellious thoughts in the hearts of some lest they should be turned to better things and *be saved.* The hosts of Midian are prowling round us now on the holy ground. A choir boy is tempted to look away from his book to smile at a neighbour, and he loses his place, and sings the wrong verse of the psalm; Satan has come also, and desires to turn God's praise into mockery. The preacher enters the pulpit, and preaches earnestly and well, and the people listen spell-bound to his words. Satan comes also, even into the pulpit, and suggests thoughts of pride to the preacher's heart. A saint of old after preaching was once highly complimented : " What a grand sermon," said his friends, and he answered, " the devil told me that before I left the pulpit." Even at the Altar of the Blessed Sacrament Satan comes also. There we come close to Jesus, yet we may be parted from Him. The two thieves at the Crucifixion come equally near to Jesus, yet the one was saved, the other lost. So two people kneel together at Holy Communion, both are equally near to Jesus, both receive His Body and Blood ; the one with earnest faith and fixed thought sees Jesus verily, and receives Him into his heart ; the other careless, and thinking of other things, sees worldly pleasure, and earthly care floating in the very cup of Christ's dear Blood ; and the one is satisfied with good things, the other is sent empty away. Satan has come also, trying to drag souls away from life, away from Jesus. Hence

come our wandering thoughts in prayer, our dull, cold
Bible-reading, our useless attendance at Church ; Satan
is prowling on the holy ground, and we have not resisted
him. Hear the wise man's advice, " Keep thy foot when
thou goest to the House of God, and be more ready to
hearken than to give the sacrifice of fools." When you
are upon the holy ground remember that Satan comes
there also, and be on your guard. Fight against the
enemies of your soul,

> " Smite them by the merit
> Of the holy Cross."

Cry out to Jesus in the hour of your weakness. Try to
picture Him hanging upon the Cross. Try to realise the
sight of His dear Feet and Hands bleeding for *you*; cling
to the Crucified in prayer, then even Satan cannot harm
you, for he trembles before the Cross, even as Dagon fell
before the Ark of God.

> " Christian, dost thou feel them,
> How they work within,
> Striving, tempting, luring,
> Goading into sin ?"

Our worst enemies are inside us, because Satan puts
evil thoughts into our hearts unless we keep them as
sanctuaries of the Holy Ghost. We go, perhaps, to some
scene of innocent amusement, where young people are
enjoying themselves. Satan comes also. He directs a

woman's eye to a neighbour's dress, and fills her heart
with the sin of envy. People are talking together, and
Satan suggests some cruel speech about another's character. When the guests sit down to table, Satan comes
also ; he passes the wine cup round faster and faster, till
the devil of drunkenness is aroused in men's hearts.
Young men and women meet in innocent companionship,
Satan comes also, and suggests the impure thought, and
the impure word—" luring into sin." Or a man meets
with a terrible sorrow, he loses some one very dear to
him, or he loses his money, and then Satan comes also,
and tells him that God is cruel and unjust : " God allows
you to be ruined, permits you to starve, where is the use
of trusting in Him, curse God and die." Thus Satan
speaks, " goading into sin."

Dear brethren, do not be downhearted, if our flesh
tempts us with unholy thoughts, let us mortify our flesh ;
let us use such abstinence that our flesh may be subdued
to the spirit.

> " Christian, never tremble,
> Never be downcast,
> Smite them by the virtue
> Of the Lenten fast."

But Satan does not always attack us in the guise of an
enemy, he "speaks us fair," and then he is most dangerous.
It was said of old, " I fear the Greeks, especially when

they bring gifts ;" specially ought we to fear Satan when he comes as a friend.

> " Christian, dost thou hear them,
> How they speak thee fair ?
> ' Always fast and vigil ?
> Always watch and prayer ?' "

Satan speaks some of us fair, and lets us believe that religion is a very good thing, that Church-going is quite right, that prayer and fasting are useful. He will not frighten us by coming as a fiend, he assumes the form of an angel of light, and whispers, " always fast and vigil ?" He tells us that we should rest a little, we have had a hard week's work, why should we go to Church on Sunday morning ? especially, why should we rise early to go to Holy Communion. Next week will do quite as well. Or he tells us that the weather is stormy, and that we had better stay at home instead of going to Church, although we know that no amount of stormy weather would keep us from our business. Dear brethren, Satan has spoken to you in this way over and over again, and you have listened sometimes. For the future,

> " Christian, answer boldly,
> While I breathe, I pray."

Satan trembles when he sees a Christian on his knees. I know very well, as you know, that this battle of ours is a very hard one, that this watching and struggling with temptation is very bitter at times, but some one else knows it also. Jesus knows your sorrows.

> " Well I know your trouble,
>   O my servant true,
>   Thou art very weary,
>   I was weary too."

Yes, He who was tempted in the wilderness, He whose sweat dropped like blood in Gethsemane, He who fought out the bitter battle on Calvary Cross, He knows your troubles, and will strengthen you for the fight. " Only be strong, and of a good courage," bear the toil, and fight the good fight to the end, since Jesus tells you,

> " That toil shall make thee
>   Some day all mine own,
>   And the end of sorrow
>   Shall be near my throne."

" ' Christian, seek not yet repose,'
  Hear thy guardian angel say,
  Thou art in the midst of foes;
              ' Watch and pray.'

" Principalities and powers,
  Mustering their unseen array,
  Wait for thy unguarded hours :
              ' Watch and. pray.'

" Gird thy heavenly armour on,
  Wear it ever night and day ;
  Ambushed lies the Evil one ;
              ' Watch and pray.'

" Hear the victors who o'ercame ;
  Still they mark each warrior's way ;
  All with one sweet voice exclaim,
              ' Watch and pray.'

" Hear, above all, hear thy Lord,
  Him thou lovest to obey ;
  Hide within thy heart His Word,
              ' Watch and pray.'

" Watch, as if on that alone,
  Hung the issue of the day ;
  Pray, that help may be sent down ;
              ' Watch and pray.' '

SERMON IV.

The Warfare.

(LENT).

ST. MATTHEW XXVI. 41.

" Watch and pray."

I HAVE told you that the warfare which we have to wage is a spiritual warfare; a fight against fallen angels far more powerful, more swift and intelligent than ourselves. The one desire of these enemies is to shut us out of that Heaven which they have forfeited. We have seen that these foes, countless in number, fight against us in different ways, entering even into the holiest places, and trying first one temptation and then another.

> " ' Christian, seek not yet repose,'
> Hear thy guardian angel say :
> ' Thou art in the midst of foes ;
>   Watch and pray.'

> " Principalities and powers,
> Mustering their unseen array ;
> Wait for thy unguarded hours ;
>   ' Watch and pray.' "

From this battle there is no escape, from this hard service there is no discharge. We must either fight, or be taken prisoner by the enemy. We must either be Christ's soldiers, or the devil's slaves. And this warfare is a life-long battle, it is not equally severe at all times; but there is no period when we may safely lay aside our weapons or our armour; there is no time when we may safely neglect our watch.

> " Gird thy heavenly armour on,
> Wear it ever night and day ;
> Ambushed lies the Evil one ;
>   ' Watch and pray.' "

Let us think, then, who helps us in this hard warfare, who is on our side. We could never fight the battle alone. Our enemies are far too numerous and too powerful for us to resist unaided. Who, then, is on our side ? First of all, Jesus is with us.

Jesus came and took our flesh upon Him, and in that flesh He fought with Satan and conquered him. Not only in the wilderness, but throughout His earthly life Jesus was tempted as Man. He came on earth to give us a perfect pattern for our life ; and as the human life of Christ was one of constant struggle against the attacks of Satan, so must our life be. Jesus carried our human nature triumphantly through this battle, through death, through a glorious resurrection ; thus giving us a pledge that He will do the same for us. He gives us an assurance that those who are His people, who still hold closely to Him, who fight in the strength which He gives, shall come safely through all ; though often sorely tried, often badly wounded, often weary and heart-sick, and heavy laden, often downcast and sad, yet conquerors at last, crowned with victory in that Heavenly Jerusalem, where temptations come not.

Remember then, brethren, Jesus is with you in the battle ; One who knows your trials and temptations ; One who has fought a good fight Himself; One who *loves* you; One who will not suffer you to be tempted above what you are able to bear. Who else is on our side ? The Holy Angels are with us in the fight. As the evil angels desire our ruin, so the holy angels, who ever do God's will, desire our happiness and salvation. "Are they not all ministering spirits sent forth to minister to such as shall be heirs of salvation ?" And who are these heirs of salvation ? We who have been baptized in Christ's holy Church. We who have been made children of God, and inheritors of the kingdom of Heaven. Every baptized person who is thus made God's child has a guardian angel appointed to watch over him, to guide him, to fight for him in the battle.

> " ' Christian, seek not yet repose,'
> Hear thy guardian angel say."

When at the font you were brought to Jesus as a little

child, there stood by you, all unseen, a watcher and a
holy one, an angel, who will never leave you unless you
go over to Satan, and forsake God utterly. Because we
cannot see our guardian angel, there is no reason for us
to disbelieve in its presence. We cannot see God, or
Heaven, yet we believe in both. We know, too, from
our Bible that many persons have seen angels, and it is
very common for dying people, who see far more clearly
into the unknown world than we who stay on earth, to
tell us that they can discern these messengers of God.
Think of this, my brethren, and learn to say—

> " My soul, there is a country
> Far beyond the stars,
> Where stands a winged sentry,
> All skilful in the wars.
> There, above all noise and danger,
> Sweet Peace sits crowned with smiles ;
> And One born in a manger
> Commands the beauteous files."

Learn to believe that God has sent His holy angel to
minister to you during your life. When you are out in
the fields at your work, the angel is beside you, when you
are engaged in your domestic concerns at home the angel
is with you. The angel of your child watches over its
cradle. *Your* angel watches over you. When you say
or do anything wrong you grieve that holy watcher whom
God has sent to you. But above all you have the com-

fort of knowing that the holy angels fight against your spiritual foes. There is ever this battle between good and evil going on in the world, and in each one of our hearts. At times we are forced to cry out, like the prophet's servant, " Alas, my Master, how shall we do ?" But the comforting answer comes, "Fear not, for they that be with us are more than they which be with them."

But remember this, that if we are to have God's angels with us we must strive to live as God's people. We must take care of what we do and say, " because of the angels." If we go on sinning deliberately, never trying to do better, we drive away the Holy Spirit from us, and then our guardian angel flies away, and leaves us to our fate. Thus far we have seen that in our warfare we have God and the holy angels on our side. But more than this, we have the prayers of the Saints to help us.

> " Hear the victors who o'ercame ;
>   Still they mark each warrior's way;
>   All with one sweet voice exclaim,
>   ' Watch and pray.' "

The whole Church of Christ, that part which is still militant here in earth, and that part which is resting in Paradise, prays for us. You know that in the Church services we always pray for each other, for the whole Church. We say, " give *us* grace to withstand the temptations of the world, the flesh, and the devil ;"

c

" graft in *our* hearts the love of Thy name;" so at this moment wherever two or three are gathered together in Church, they are praying for us. And in the Church in Paradise the holy men and women of all ages, who have entered into their rest, pray for us who are still fighting the battle here in earth. Take courage, then, and take comfort. Be brave, be strong, remember who fights on your side. "Be strong and of a good courage, and the Lord He it is that doth go before thee."

" Hear, above all, hear thy Lord,
Him thou lovest to obey ;
Hide within thy heart His Word,
    ' Watch and pray.'

" Watch, as if on that alone,
Hung the issue of the day ;
Pray, that help may be sent down ;
    ' Watch and pray.'"

" Soldiers, who are Christ's below,
    Strong in faith resist the foe;
    Boundless is the pledged reward
    Unto them who serve the Lord.

" 'Tis no palm of fading leaves
    That the conquerors' hand receives ;
    Joys are his, serene and pure,
    Light that ever shall endure.

" For the souls that overcome
    Waits the beauteous heavenly home,
    Where the Blessed evermore
    Tread, on high, the starry floor.

" Passing soon and little worth
    Are the things that tempt on earth ;
    Heavenward lift thy soul's regard,
    God Himself is thy reward.

" Father, who the crown dost give,
    Saviour, by whose death we live,
    Spirit, who our hearts dost raise,
    Three in One, Thy Name we praise."

SERMON V.

The Warfare.

(LENT).

REVELATION III. 21.

" To him that overcometh."

WE have seen the nature of our spiritual warfare, the foes with whom we have to deal, and the friends who aid us. Next let me tell you how we are to fight, and with what weapons. How are we to fight the battle ? First, *with patience and steadfastness.*

> " Soldiers, who are Christ's below,
> Strong in faith resist the foe ;
> Boundless is the pledged reward
> Unto them who serve the Lord."

Our warfare is a life-long battle, and thus it will not do for us to be brave one day, and cowardly the next. It will not do for us to fight hard at one time with prayer and self-examination, and then to be careless and neglect-ful. We must strive to be *patient* in running the race, and in fighting the battle ; remembering on the one hand, how deadly is the hatred, and how great the cunning, of our foes, and on the other hand, how infinitely greater is the love of God, and how far more the prayers of the saints prevail than the wiles of Satan. Strengthened in this way, the weakest will be made sufficient for the battle ; for we know that even tender women and delicate little children have overcome the temptations of the world, and the fury of their enemies in the strength given them from above. When you wake in the morning prepare for the battle. Look on the day before you as one to be passed in a battle field. There are very few people who will not have at least one struggle with sin before the day is ended. Picture to yourselves the dark ranks of your foes, Satan's angels, sending forth their arrows, even bitter words, evil fancies, impure thoughts, temptations of all kinds. These will fight with you *to-day.* Then look on those who fight for you.

Picture Jesus, your Brother, wearing your flesh, knowing your weakness, helping you in your need. Picture your guardian angel standing beside you. Think of the prayers of all saints, of the whole Church, going up for you like a great cloud of incense. Then prepare yourself for the day's battle. How? *On your knees.* Kneel down, and think of the battle, of the hatred of the enemy, of the prize for which they contend—*your soul.* Then cry out to God to help you, to lead you, to strengthen you—" Lord, direct my goings in the way. Hold Thou me up that my footsteps slide not. Forsake me not, Lord God of my help." Thus praying, go forth to your battle, feeling, "they compass me about on every side, but in the name of the Lord will I destroy them." Thus you see, brethren, that you must fight your battle patiently and steadfastly every day ; and your chief weapon will be *Prayer*—never be without that. Let your motto be, "whilst I breathe, I pray." To-day when the bad thought comes, when the angry word rises, when the temptation to say or do something wrong comes, *think*—the enemy is fighting with me now, now the Philistines be upon me ; then fly to your weapon, Prayer ; cry out to God, with your heart, if not with your voice, " Lord, help me *now*; Jesus, Master, have mercy upon me."

Next, *we must fight, watching, and distrusting ourselves.* If you knew that robbers were coming to attack your house on a certain night, you would watch. You would make the doors and windows fast, you would call in help, and have armed men ready. But very often you don't do this against the worst of all robbers, Satan, who wants to rob you of your soul, to defraud you of Heaven. The doors and windows are often left wide open, the eye is open to see a bad sight, the heart is open for a bad thought to enter, the tongue is left unguarded. There are no weapons ready, and suddenly the enemy comes when least expected, and robs you of your innocence, or your purity, or your peace of mind. I say then unto you all, Watch ; " Watch and pray, lest ye enter into temptation."

And next, do not trust yourselves. Do not think that

you are too respectable to be tempted, or too well brought up, or too regular a Church-goer to fall away. Don't trust yourselves, but watch yourselves. Have perfect trust in God, and doubt yourselves. When we think we are strongest, we are often most weak. The devil sometimes leaves us for a time that we may fall asleep, that our weapons may grow rusty. Then our prayers are neglected, our self-examination given up, our watchfulness omitted, and just at the most unguarded moment comes the blow, and we fall. Never suppose because we are sleeping that Satan is asleep also. I have heard of an old man who said to an aged neighbour, " I am dead to the world." " Then," answered his friend, " do not trust yourself till you are out of the world, for if you are dead, the devil is not." We need this constant watchfulness in our battle because Satan does not always fight in one way. He tries all kinds of attacks, and various sorts of weapons. As Ishbi-benob, the giant, took a new sword when he saw David waxing faint, and thought to have slain him, so Satan ever and anon takes a new sword against us. He sees some of us getting faint and weary of the battle, neglecting our watch, laying aside our armour; then he strikes us with a new sword, a fresh temptation, and wounds our souls. He has been trying some of you, perhaps, with the temptation to be angry, or discontented, or to say foolish words, or to think bad thoughts; and you have fought bravely against this temptation, and have conquered. You have felt that it is well with you, that you have got the better of your bad habit, and then Satan has come with a new sword. He sends the temptation of *pride;* he leads us to think how good we are, how much better than our neighbours, and then if we are not prepared, we are wounded grievously. Perhaps Satan has tempted you to keep away from Church, and to neglect prayer, and you have fought against this temptation, and have come to Church. Then the tempter takes a new sword; he puts some foolish or wrong thought into your mind, and instead of getting help and comfort from the service, your thoughts wander away from God. Then Satan knows that his new sword has struck home, you have come to Church, but he has wounded you even there.

Take heed then, dear brethren, for the enemy is doubtless preparing a new sword for you now. You have been in earnest this Lent, you have looked into your way of life, have examined the secret chambers of your hearts, you have repented of some sin. Now take care of the re-action. Soon the joyful Eastertide will be here. The gloomy days of Lent will be ended. There will be a time of holiday-keeping, when friends and neighbours meet together. Then the devil will be busy, he will be waiting to wound you. If he finds you careless after the serious thoughts of Lent, if he finds you neglecting your prayers and your duties, he will try you first with one sword, then with another. He will try one with the sword of strong drink, another with the sword of bad company, and then with the sword of bad talk, *be on your guard.* Satan comes to us when we least expect him. Judas was with the Apostles, Moses was working a miracle, Cain was offering a sacrifice, Jonah was going to preach, when the whisper of the Tempter came.

Be brave then, dear friends, and fight on. You will grow stronger, and the enemy weaker, the longer you fight. Cling close to Jesus in prayer and in the Blessed Sacrament, and you shall conquer. Then think of the reward promised " to him that overcometh."

> " 'Tis no palm of fading leaves
>   That the conqueror's hand receives ;
>   Joys are his, serene and pure,
>   Light that ever shall endure."

For those who have overcome *themselves,* who have conquered passion and anger, and lust ; who have tried hard to quit themselves like men, and fight, enduring hardness as good soldiers of Jesus Christ, for them is laid up the crown formed of the pure gold of God's perfect love, and studded with the priceless jewels of peace, and joy, and contentment. For them is prepared the white robe never more to be spotted with sin, even the righteousness of Saints; and after the agony of Gethsemane and the battle on Calvary, they shall find rest with Jesus, even " the rest that remaineth to the people of God."

" Ten thousand times ten thousand,
   In sparkling raiment bright,
   The armies of the ransomed saints
   Throng up the steeps of light :
   'Tis finished ! all is finished,
   Their fight with death and sin ;
   Fling open wide the golden gates,
   And let the victors in.

" What rush of Alleluias
   Fills all the earth and sky !
   What ringing of a thousand harps
   Bespeak the triumph nigh !
   O day, for which creation
   And all its tribes were made !
   O joy, for all its former woes
   A thousand-fold repaid !

" Oh, then what raptured greetings
   On Canaan's happy shore,
   What knitting severed friendships up,
   Where partings are no more !
   Then eyes with joy shall sparkle.
   That brimmed with tears of late ;
   Orphans no longer fatherless,
   Nor widows desolate.

" Bring near Thy great salvation,
   Thou Lamb for sinners slain,
   Fill up the roll of Thine elect,
   Then take Thy power and reign ;
   Appear, Desire of nations,
   Thine exiles long for home ;
   Show in the Heavens Thy promised sign ;
   Thou Prince and Saviour, come."

SERMON VI.

The Bright Morning.

(EASTER.)

REVELATION XXI. 4.

" God shall wipe away all tears from their eyes."

A LITTLE boy lay dying. The weeping friends around the little bed knew that the end was very near. Presently the child turned his wan face to his mother, and whispered, " My doctor will come soon; I shall be better in the morning." He was right. That night Jesus, the Good Physician, came and took him home, and he was better, aye, well, in the morning. " Sorrow may endure for a night, but joy cometh in the morning." And so with us, we are all troubled in one way or another. Some are sick with sin, others sick with sorrow. Some eyes are dim with weeping, others with old age. Some of us have aching limbs, many of us have aching hearts. Some are poor and needy, some lonely and forsaken. But whatever our ailment be, if we are Christ's people, we shall be better in the morning. " The night is far spent, the day is at hand," and we shall be better in the morning.

" On the resurrection morning
    Soul and body meet again,
    No more sorrow, no more weeping,
    No more pain."

Here is the blessed message of comfort which Easter brings to us. We must find sorrow here, pain, trouble, disappointment, death. But after death comes the resurrection. The night of the grave is followed by the morn of resurrection, and we shall be better in the morning. Some of you, perhaps, have seen a beautiful picture, called "*the first Easter dawn*," which represents two angels flying, and shading their eyes to catch the first glimpse of the Easter Dawn. It is very early in the morning, the bare crosses of Good Friday still stand out dark against the sky, and there is a golden light in the east, which tells of the resurrection of Jesus, the Sun of righteousness, rising with healing in his wings.

Ah ! my brethren, some of us are straining our eyes through the gloom of this world to catch a glimpse of the bright morning to come. We, too, can see the crosses where we have suffered with Jesus ; crosses of pain, of want, or of sickness. We can see the grave where we buried our dear ones, and perhaps our joy along with them. But beyond all these, beyond the cross, and the grave, beyond the heart-ache and the pain, the eye of faith can see the light of hope, the light of the resurrection morning; "because Jesus has risen, we shall rise also;" "joy cometh in the morning."

> " Saints, your cross in patience bearing,
> Mourners, stained with many a tear,
> Penitents, in sorrow wearing
> Darkest weeds of shame and fear ;
> Christ is risen ! Lose your sadness,
> Joying with the joyous throng,
> Faithful hearts will find their gladness
> Joining in the Easter song.
> Christ is risen ! Risen, brother,
> Brother, Christ is risen indeed !"

How shall we speak of the wonders of the resurrection morning? How shall we describe the joys of Heaven? Painters have tried to picture those glories, poets have sung of them, enthusiasts have dreamed of them, but all have failed to realise them. Even the inspired words of S. John fail to describe fully the City of our God. How can man, laden with earth, fly, even in thought, up to Heaven? And yet we yearn to do so, as the eagle soars up towards the sun, though beaten back by its fierce glory. We can but catch, like Moses, a far-off glimpse of the Promised Land, since " eye hath not seen, nor ear heard, neither have entered into the heart of man, the things which God hath prepared for them that love Him."

What does the Hymn before us tell us of Heaven?

First, it tells us of the conquerors who enter Heaven.

> " 'Tis finished !   All is finished,
>   Their fight with death and sin ;
>   Fling open wide the golden gates,
>   And let the victors in."

Jesus, the Captain of our Salvation, rose from the dead, and ascended up on high, leading captivity captive. He, the true Samson, went down to Hades, the city of Satan, the Philistine, the enemy of souls ; thence he arose, bearing off the gates of that gloomy Gaza, " for he hath broken the gates of brass, and cut the bars of iron asunder." Death and Hell are robbed of their victims. Death had held all men in bondage, but Jesus rose to raise all men up, and the gates of Hell shall not prevail against them. Thus Jesus arose and went to His Father ; and then came the Angels' shout of triumph—" lift up you heads, O ye gates, and be ye lifted up ye everlasting doors, and the King of Glory shall come in." And so for us " a door was opened in Heaven." And at the end of the world, on the resurrection morning, He who has come to judge us will once more ascend with all the multitude of His redeemed, with all His saints, from those at the beginning of the world, to those whose names were last written in the Book of Life. The noble army of martyrs, and all the victor throng will enter through the gates into the city with their Captain. It is a grand sight even on earth to look at an army of conquerors. I saw the troops come home from the Crimea, and watched miles of bright bayonets as regiment after regiment marched by; men who had fought at Alma and Inkerman, men who had ridden in the death-ride at Balaklava, men who had lain in the freezing trenches before Sebastopol. Hearts throbbed, and eyes flashed as those conquerors went by. But what must be the sight in Heaven, when high and low, rich and poor, walk in one grand procession, bearing the palms of victory; of victory over sin, victory over self, victory over pride or falsehood!

The king will be there, who by his prayers conquered the evil in his kingdom; and there, too, will be the poor widow who gave her mite to Jesus, and was thankful. The martyrs who conquered by faith, when the lions mangled them in the arena; the little child who gave up its own will for the sake of others; all who have fought a good fight, and kept the faith, will be there, "clothed in white raiment, and palms in their hands,"—

> " Fling open wide the golden gates,
> And let the victors in."

" 'Tis finished, all is finished :" there shall be no more struggles with temptation, no more bitter battles with sin; the hand that wielded the sword clasps the palm now; the soldier, "weary with the march of life," rests his feet on the green pastures of the Better Land.

Next, the Hymn tells of the triumph song of Heaven.

> " What rush of Alleluias
> Fills all the earth and sky."

D

We all know the wondrous power of music here on earth. When soldiers hang back weary and dispirited, the band plays, and they rush forward to the charge. When our spirit is disturbed, and our hearts feel sad, a soft strain of music will often bring comfort to us, as David's harp did to Saul. How full of rest and peace is the quiet time spent in some vast cathedral, where we listen to the anthem pealing through the dim aisles, till it dies away among the echoes! I remember once when I was holding a service on the upper deck of an Emigrant ship one Good Friday, how the people, who were going away from the old country for ever, sang " Rock of Ages." At first only a few voices were heard, but gradually one after another took up the dear old words, and a great wave of sound rose up through the cold March air, and passers by on the river checked their boats to listen in wonder. Every heart was touched by that simple hymn.

But what must the music of Heaven be like, where all who on earth sang the Lord's song in a strange land, shall sing it anew in His presence, with hearts and voices alike in tune! Those who sang in trained choirs amid the " dim religious light " of the Minster, the old who quavered out "Guide me, O Thou great Redeemer," with feeble voice, but with strong faith, these shall join in the song of Heaven, and sing, perchance, the same loved hymns as of old. Musicians tell us that on earth no instrument is ever perfectly in tune; but in Heaven all things will be in tune to sing the one great song, the praise of Jesus, our Brother, who was dead, and is alive again, was lost, and is found.

Again, the Hymn tells of the meetings in Heaven.

There will be the meeting of parent and child. The little ones who clung round their father's knee like flowers springing at the foot of a forest oak, and who went before us into the silent land; the bright boy, the only son of his mother, the gentle girl who faded away with the fatal beauty of consumption on her face, these we shall meet again. Augustine shall once more kneel by the side of Monica, and murmur to his Lord, "I loved thee late, but not too late for pardon."* And many another good mother shall hear the words spoken—"Your schooling led me here."

There, too, will be the meeting of friends,—

> " What knitting severed friendships up,
> Where partings are no more."

Once more Jonathan will clasp the hand of David, and think not of the bloody fight at Gilboa. Moses will have crossed the river at last, and Joshua will be there to meet him. Those who loved us and were true to us, those with whom we took sweet counsel on earth, will meet us in Heaven, and we shall walk together in the House of God as friends. Sometimes when friends meet on earth

* "Sero te amavi." *Augustine.*

after long years of separation, time and trouble have so
altered them that we scarcely know them again ; but how
much greater will be the change in Heaven ! And yet I
believe we shall know our friends, though the dear face
which we remember scarred and wasted with disease will
be all healthful then. The crippled limbs, the blinded
eyes, the deaf ears, will be all cured there, where the
Good Physician dwells. The eyes of the poor mourner,
so often dim with weeping here, will be bright with
happiness there, for " God shall wipe away all tears from
their eyes." There will be no need to look for the tears
of Ruth,

> " When, sick for home,
> She stood in tears amid the alien corn."

She has gone home long ago, and has found Naomi
again, and all tears are wiped away. Mary need weep
no more for Lazarus, but may sit once more at the feet
of Jesus. S. John can lie once more on that dear breast,
and fear no malice of the traitor. And we, if we love our
dear Lord now, and try humbly and earnestly to do His
will, shall find a place in Heaven ; we, too, shall meet
the loving glance of those dear eyes ; we, too, shall hear
sweet words of praise for our poor efforts,—" well done,
good and faithful servants."

As I look at the quiet Churchyard, and " the grassy
barrows of the happier dead," I feel how true are those
words, " the *Harvest* is the end of the world." Oh !

may it be truly said of each of us one day, " Lord, if he sleep he shall do well." Yea, if we sleep in the Lord, we shall indeed do well, since we know of a truth,

> " When 'neath the sod
>   I have slept long, my God
>   Will wake me up."

" Come, Thou Holy Spirit, come ;
  And from Thy celestial home
  Shed a ray of light Divine ;
  Come, Thou Father of the poor,
  Come, Thou source of all our store,
  Come, within our bosoms shine.

" Thou of Comforters the best,
  Thou the soul's most welcome guest,
  Sweet refreshment here below ;
  In our labour rest most sweet,
  Grateful coolness in the heat,
  Solace in the midst of woe.

" O most Blessed Light Divine,
  Shine within these hearts of Thine,
  And our inmost spirits fill ; ·
  Where Thou art not, man hath nought,
  Nothing good in deed or thought,
  Nothing free from taint of ill.

" Heal our wounds, our strength renew ;
  On our dryness pour Thy dew ;
  Wash the stains of guilt away :
  Bend the stubborn heart and will ;
  Melt the frozen, warm the chill ;
  Guide the steps that go astray. ,

" On the faithful, who adore
  And confess Thee, evermore
  In Thy sevenfold gifts descend :
  Give them virtue's sure reward,
  Give them Thy salvation, Lord,
  Give them joys that never end."

SERMON VII.

A Man's Life.

S. LUKE XII. 15.

" A man's life consisteth not in the abundance of the things which he possesseth."

A MAN'S life ! Every thoughtful man will find much to think about in those few words. A man's life ;—whence comes it, whither does it go, what can be done with it ? Or as individuals we may think—my life, what is it, what am I making of it, what did God intend it to be ? Now, life is the gift of God, the life of the body and the life of the soul both come from Him. " In the beginning God formed man out of the dust of the ground, and breathed into his nostrils the breath of life, and man became a living soul." Life, then, comes from God. We can destroy the life of the body, but we cannot give it. We can kill an insect, or a man, but we cannot restore them to life, nor can we prolong life when the time for death has come. Since, then, life is lent to us by God, we may not throw it away recklessly, as a gambler does money, but we must use it carefully, looking to the future, as a farmer uses his seed.

This subject of a man's life is a very wide one. I will only take one or two points now as showing what a man's life *is not*, and what *it is ;* and as specially bearing on the teaching of the day, when true life was given to the Christian Church by the Holy Ghost, who is the Lord, and Giver of Life. The text tells us *what a man's life is not.* "A man's life consisteth not in the abundance of the things which he possesseth." It is a very common mistake to suppose that a true life is a successful life, a prosperous and wealthy man is said to have succeeded *in life.* But that is not the sort of life to which Jesus refers in the text. He shows us in one place the picture of a man who had been prosperous, one who wore purple and fine linen, and fared sumptuously every day; one whom many had envied. Yet his life was not a success, and there are none of us who would care to change places with him. The Gospel also shows us another example of a mistaken life. It shows us a young ruler who had great possessions, and many good qualities, yet his life was not a success: he went away from the true Life, he went away from Jesus. No, "a man's life consisteth not in the abundance of the things which he possesseth." It matters not whether we are rich or poor, successful or unfortunate, clever or dull; the secret of a true life consists in trying to do our duty towards God and our neighbour in that station of life to which it has pleased God to call us. This is the only true life, the only life worth living, the only life which brings comfort here, and happiness hereafter, since " the path of duty is the way to glory." Some one has said very truly, " The word DUTY seems to me the biggest word in the world, and is uppermost in all my serious doings." When Lord Nelson lay dying, in the hour of his last great victory, at Trafalgar, his last words were "thank God, I have done my duty." Believe me, brethren, his is the only true life who can say at the last, feeling all his failures and mistakes, and humbly conscious of his weakness, " thank God, I have *tried* to do my duty." There is only one path for us to tread in as Christian people, and that is the path of duty marked out for us by God.

> " He that walks it, only thirsting
> For the right, and learns to deaden
> Love of self ; before his journey closes,
> He shall find the stubborn thistle bursting
> Into glossy purples, which out-redden
> All voluptuous garden roses."

It is related of a certain famous statesman, that in the early days of photography, he was about to have his portrait taken. The operator begged him to keep perfectly steady for a moment, but he moved, and in consequence

there was only a blur where a great man's likeness ought
to have appeared. How many people, from want of a
steadfast attention to their duty, present to the eyes
of the world merely a blur, instead of the picture of a
noble life ! I have said that the true life is *the life of
duty.* And that life, if truly carried out, will be an *earnest
life.* No one succeeds unless he is in earnest. This is
true of every calling and walk in life. If you look into
the ranks of men who have succeeded, the great dis-
coverers, the great men of science, the famous painters,
sculptors or soldiers, you will find that they were in
earnest ; that they began and persevered, often with little
or no encouragement.

We look at a certain boy, making a rude laboratory in
his garret, at Penzance, and by-and-bye we find that boy
grown into the great chemist, Humphrey Davy. Or we
read of another boy, working in a cook's shop, and
drawing pictures in flour and charcoal on the walls, and
presently we find him known as Claude Lorraine, the first
landscape painter of his age. These men were in *earnest.*
So it is with all work, from the meanest to the grandest,
to do it well we must be in earnest. If a labourer is set
to clear a field of weeds, and if he is in earnest, he takes
two hands to his work. So if we are to get rid of the
weeds of evil habits and besetting sins, if we are to sweep
the house, and search diligently till we find the precious
treasure which we have lost, we must put two hands to

the work. Every man who wants to live a true life, must
have a definite object, and be in earnest in reaching it.
Those who succeed are those who aim high. The school-
boy who is contented with the second place in his class
will never be first. The man who is content to sleep in
the valley will never reach the mountain-top of success.
Of course our aims in life are very different. One determines to be a great preacher, another a successful
merchant; one desires to be a good farmer, another a
clever mechanic. One woman has the power of helping
suffering humanity, and becomes a Florence Nightingale,
or a Sister Dora. Another has no wider sphere of work
than a labourer's cottage. But whatever our work is, if
we are to succeed we must be in earnest, we must do it
with our might. Never be ashamed of your work or
position ; if it be a humble calling, raise it and glorify it
by honesty and faithfulness in discharging it. Has not
Jesus sanctified labour in the Nazareth workshop? It
has been well said that there is nothing to be ashamed of
in being a shoemaker, but there is something to be
ashamed of in making a bad shoe. But, brethren, the
highest life is not the earnest working for success. I tell
you to be in earnest in worldly matters, but do not put
them first. As Christian people your highest aim should
be to do your duty towards God. This life is for all men
a time of fighting and struggling, and working, and plan-
ning; made up of actions, thoughts, and longings, great

and small, good and bad. Our aim should be to bring this life into subjection to God's will ; so that we may consecrate it to Him who has bought us with His Precious Blood. As the Israelites saw the marks of the Passover blood on their door-posts, and knew that they were saved, so should we ever see the marks of Christ's redeeming Blood upon us, and feel that we are not our own, that our life is not our own, that our time is not our own, and that our duty is to say, " Lo, I come to do Thy Will, O Lord." Thus far we have seen that "a man's life consisteth not in the abundance of the things which he possesseth." He may be rich or poor, this is only an accident. A true life is one of duty towards God and our neighbour, done earnestly and with our might ; a life which aims at Heaven, a life whose ruling principle is the Will of God. And again, the true life is not only an earnest life, but also an *unselfish life.* God will not only have us good ourselves, but will have us make others good. We all influence our fellow-men for good or evil, just as we ourselves are good or evil. A bad man in a parish or community is like a plague-spot, he is not only bad himself, but he makes others bad. A good man in a similar place is like a sweet flower in a garden, beautiful in himself, and by shedding sweetness around him making the lives of others beautiful. Believe me, the best sermon is the example of a good life. Brethren, have you learned to look at your life in this way? Most of us, all of us indeed, must confess that our lives are not altogether satisfactory. There is too much of self, and too little of God in them. There is abundance of earnestness for the things of this life, and too little for eternity. I have read of a boy in a Sunday School who when asked if his father were a Christian, answered, " Yes, he is a Christian, but he is not working much at it just now." How true that is of many of us. When we see the lives of some who bear the name and sign of Christ's people, when we mark how faint and languid is their interest in spiritual things, we are forced to believe though they have the profession of a Christian they are not working much at it. How then, you ask, may we live the true life of which I have spoken? I will tell you. We need a model, and the means of imitating it. The model life is that of Jesus Christ, as revealed to us in the Gospel; since Jesus came into the world not only to die for us, but to show us how to live, and He ever lives now to make intercession for us, and so to help us to live the true life of His redeemed ones. We too often forget what Christ is doing *now* for us, too much religious teaching never goes beyond Calvary. Jesus promised to send the Holy Ghost to direct His Church into all holiness. If the Holy Ghost directs and rules our hearts we can make our life, however humble, a good life, a noble life, acceptable to God. Now, as you know, the Holy Ghost was first given to the Christian Church on the Day of Pentecost, that first

Whit-Sunday of old. Many persons seem to think that the gift is never repeated now. But the outpouring of the Holy Spirit on the Church, both as a body and as individuals, is constantly being repeated. The Holy Spirit comes to us in the Sacraments, otherwise they would be useless. He comes to us in holy Confirmation, otherwise that sacred rite would have no meaning. He comes to His Ministers in the solemn rite of Ordination ; and to all His people in the services of His Church. God the Holy Ghost will come to each of you, filling you more and more with all fulness if you ask with faith. The clay cottage of our body becomes the temple of the Holy Ghost, if only we will have Him to dwell there. Without that Presence, without that indwelling of the Spirit, we cannot live the true life of a Christian ; since "every good gift, and every perfect gift is from above." And the greatest of these gifts is the gift of the Holy Spirit, who gives us the power to lead a gentle, pure, unselfish life. Let us, who feel how much there is to amend in our lives, pray to-night that the precious gift of the first Whit-Sunday may be repeated now.

> " Come, Thou Holy Spirit, come ;
> And from Thy celestial home
> Shed a ray of light Divine ;
> Come, Thou Father of the poor,
> Come, Thou source of all our store,
> Come, within our bosoms shine."

Let us learn the true dignity of a life for which Christ died, since

> " A sacred burden is the life ye bear ;
> ·Look on it, lift it, bear it solemnly.
> Stand up, and walk beneath it steadfastly.
> Fail not for sorrow, falter not for sin,
> But onward, upward, till the goal ye win."

" I was a wandering sheep,
  I did not love the fold,
  I did not love my shepherd's voice,
  I would not be controlled.
  I was a wayward child,
  I did not love my home,
  I did not love my Father's voice,
  I loved afar to roam.

'' The Shepherd sought His sheep,
  The Father sought His child,
  They followed me o'er vale and hill,
  O'er deserts waste and wild ;
  They found me nigh to death,
  Famished, and faint, and lone ;
  They bound me with the bands of love,
  They saved the wandering one.

" They spoke in tender love,
  They raised my drooping head ;
  They gently closed my bleeding wounds,
  My fainting soul they fed ;
  They washed my filth away,
  They made me clean and fair ;
  They brought me to my home in peace,
  The long-sought wanderer.

" Jesus my Shepherd is,
  'Twas He that loved my soul,
  'Twas He that washed me in His Blood,
  'Twas He that made me whole ;
  'Twas He that sought the lost,
  That found the wandering sheep ;
  'Twas He that brought me to the fold,
  'Tis He that still doth keep.

" I was a wandering sheep,
  I would not be controlled ;
  But now I love my Shepherd's voice,
  I love, I love the fold.
  I was a wayward child,
  I once preferred to roam,
  But now I love my Father's voice,
  I love, I love my home."

SERMON VIII.

The Wanderer.

St. Luke xv. 17, 18.

" When he came to himself, he said, . . . I will arise, and go to my Father."

THE story of the Prodigal Son is the story of every one who has sinned grievously, and who has been led by God's mercy to repent truly; of every one who has gone away from God, and has come back again. That story is told in the hymn which we sang just now. Some of you know this sad truth from your own experience. You can remember some sin, its weight, its misery, its wretchedness. And you can remember how you repented, and went back to God. You can recall the misery of the departure, and the joy of the return. Perhaps there are some here who feel that they are still away from God, still clinging to their sin, hating it perhaps, and fearing its consequences, and yet not wise enough, nor brave enough, to arise and go home. I speak to both classes. There are four points for us to notice. The Prodigal

E

leaving home. Then the Prodigal enjoying the pleasures of sin. Then the Prodigal tasting the sorrows of sin. And lastly, the Prodigal returning home. First of all, I look at the Prodigal leaving home. Why did he leave home ? Because he wanted to be his own master, and to have his own way.

> " I was a wandering sheep,
> I did not love the fold,
> I did not love my Shepherd's voice,
> I would not be controlled.
> I was a wayward child,
> I did not love my home,
> I did not love my Father's voice,
> I loved afar to roam."

As long as a son obeys his father's commands, and attends to the wishes of others, rather than his own, all is well. He abides in his father's house, he enjoys one of the greatest of all blessings, a happy home. But when the son becomes wilful, and breaks the law of his father, and forsakes the teaching of his mother, and follows his own way, home is no longer home to him. He feels like a criminal, because he knows he is deceiving those whom he is bound to love and honour. Once he used to look his father honestly in the face, now he is afraid to meet his eye. Once he told his mother about his troubles, now he has secrets from her. He has taken the first step down hill. Soon he takes the second step

,down hill—he leaves his father's house. Now let us look at ourselves. God our Heavenly Father has given us certain laws and commandments. He says we are to do certain things, and we are *not* to do certain other things. As long as we keep His laws all is well with us. We abide in our Father's House, the Church. We are not ashamed to look our Father in the face, that is to say, we pray to Him, and tell Him our secrets. We look to His hand to feed us in the Blessed Sacrament. But when we want to go on our way, when we break His law, all is changed. And the first sign of the change is that we want to hide away from God, just as Adam tried to hide after his disobedience, and as Judas went away from Jesus, "and it was night." And we show this wish to hide from God by leaving our Father's House, the Church. We are ashamed to come to God's House bearing our guilty secret with us. I have known many sad cases of people who were once regular Communicants, and who ceased to come to the Altar. They had gone wrong, and instead of going back to their Father, they left His House, and went down hill, lower and lower. Thus you see the first wrong step is the breaking of God's law by sin, the next step is leaving the Church, our Father's House. Just as the home life is all changed for the prodigal, so our Father's House becomes changed to those who have sinned. The words of the service or sermon seem to point reproachfully to them, and to vex them and make them angry. It is home no longer to them. And so their place in Church becomes empty, their place at the Altar knows them no more, they do not pray, they *are afraid to look their Father in the face.* Next, I look at the Prodigal enjoying what he calls the pleasures of sin. Ah! yes, sin seems pleasant enough at first. To have our own way seems very delightful. Satan gives us the good wine of pleasure first, and when men have well drunken, then that which is worse. He showers roses abundantly on the sinner's path at the first, and keeps the sharp tearing thorns till later on. The devil makes the down hill road very easy at first. He is like the money-lender, who at the first makes everything pleasant for his victim. "Here is your money," he says, "you have but to sign your name here as a matter of form." But when the day of reckoning comes, the poor bankrupt finds his pleasant friend changed into a cruel taskmaster. At first the bands of sin are like the daisy chains which little children cast around them in their play, but they grow heavier and heavier, till they crush their victims like an iron shroud. The Prodigal joins himself to a citizen of that country, that country which lies outside his Father's House. In a word, he gets into bad company. He is determined to serve the devil, and the devil always finds suitable company for his slaves. When the Prodigal begins to go wrong, Satan sends him company to keep him wrong; probably some

weak or vicious woman. And for a time this company
seems very delightful. The Prodigal has his own way.
He can spend riotous evenings with his loose companions,
he rejoices that there is no father to call him to account,
or to ask him how he has spent his time. Over and over
again he repeats, " I am my own master." Not quite,
my poor friend. You have a master, even the devil, and
he is a very hard master, and by-and-bye he begins to
pay his wages. No one ever found the pleasures of sin
satisfying, and everyone finds the price paid a terrible
one. The excitement of sin makes it seem very fascinat-
ing for the time, but when we look back upon it in
calmer moments, it is but a sorry sight. Have you ever
come down early in the morning to a room where a noisy
revel was held the night before ? How different everything
looks. How grim and wretched, and " stale, flat, and
unprofitable " appears the room in the cold grey morning
light ! The lights are burned out, the wine-cup is
drained, the fire reduced to cold ashes. So looks the
morning of remorse after the night of sin. The Prodigal
begins to be in want ; to be in rags, homeless, friendless.
This was the price which he paid. The devil always
brings his servants to rags and misery at last. He begins
by offering fine clothing, and abundance of pleasure, but
the end comes in rags and misery. Look at the drunkard,
singing and laughing with his gay companions. How
merry he is ! Let us eat and drink, let the jest pass, and

the song be sung. He is well-dressed now, he has friends and money now. But by-and-bye go and see the drunkard die, as I have done. His fine clothes have gone in drink, his money, his furniture, his good name, his health have all gone in the same way. Can that miserable, blear-eyed, trembling wretch, who gropes on the floor for what is not there, can this be the same man whom we saw lately? Oh! believe me, "the way of transgressors is hard." It ends in rags, in want, in death, "for the wages of sin is death."

Look at the story of a Prodigal daughter, of a girl who leaves home, and despises the law of her mother, and breaks the covenant of her God. At first her way of life seems very pleasant. She meets with no interference. There is no mother to reprove her. Her new master, the devil, dresses her in gay clothing, and she may flaunt in jewels. How pleasant a life! Ah! wait awhile, the end is not yet. The dark time comes, and even before it comes there rises some bitterness from the very midst of her unholy pleasures. Then the dark days come, and bring illness, loneliness, shame, poverty, and above all, the memory of the past. At length she has time *to remember.* Where are the gay dresses now? Where are the wild companions now? Who will take pity upon that poor wasted body, or that poor broken heart? Rags and misery, and perhaps suicide in the black river, these things are before her—"the wages of sin is death." So we see that the pleasures of sin soon change into the sorrows of sin. Go and look at *a sinner alone with his sin;* tortured by the memories of a bad past, and by fears for an unknown future. Once he said, "I don't care," does he say so *now?* He is haunted by the ghosts of old sins,—

> "The ghosts of forgotten actions,
>   Come floating before his sight,
> And things which he thought were dead things,
>   Are alive with a terrible might.
> And the vision of all his past life
>   Is an awful thing to face,—
> Alone with his conscience sitting
>   In that solemnly silent place."

Think of the man who has led an impure life, think of him alone with his conscience, and alone with his sin, as he must be one day. What white faces of lost women must haunt him! What visions of once happy homes blighted by him must throng upon him. Does he not care *now?* Does he make light of his sins now? Such an one is in Hell already, in the Hell of hopeless terror, remorse and despair. I heard a clergyman once tell how he had been summoned to visit a man, a stranger, who was dying, and whose life had been very bad. The clergyman tried various means to arouse the man's interest in vain. He sat crouching over an empty hearth, rocking himself too and fro, and ever and again uttering in a fearful voice the one word—*Already*. The visit was repeated several times, but still the man spoke nothing but the one word, *Already;* and it was only just before the end that it was discovered that the wretched man meant that he was in *Hell Already*.

My brothers and sisters, now in your hot youth, if you are tempted to think that sin is sweet, remember the end. If you would escape the awful hours passed alone with your sin, escape now for your life. Unless you escape, you will come to spiritual destitution, to the hunger, to the husks of the Prodigal. Would that I could arouse some of you to cry now—" what must I do to be saved ?" And the answer I would give you is " go home." Make up your mind now. Determine now, " I will arise ; I will arise out of this bad company, out of this evil way ; I see my mistake, I see my danger, Father receive me. I will arise and go to my Father, and will say to him, Father, I have sinned against heaven and before Thee, and am no more worthy to be called Thy son." Will you do this *now?* There is nothing to hinder you from going home. Do you fear your reception there ? I tell you God not only waits for your return, but He meets you half way, while you are yet " a great way off."

> " The Shepherd sought His sheep,
> The Father sought His child,
> They followed me o'er vale and hill,
> O'er deserts waste and wild.

> They found me nigh to death,
> Famished, and faint, and lone ;
> They bound me with the bands of love,
> They saved the wandering one."

My brothers and sisters, if these words touch your hearts, make up your minds now. The Prodigal went home *at once*, and was forgiven. Half our good resolutions come to nothing because they are not acted upon at once. Is there anything which keeps you back ? Something which makes you ashamed to look God in the face ? *Then give it up*. Leave the bad thing behind, and go home. Don't think that your Father will not receive you. Some earthly fathers might shut the door against you, your Heavenly Father will not. Jesus, your Redeemer, is opening that door for you now. Your guardian angel is drawing you towards it now. O Prodigal Son, O Prodigal Daughter, whoever you are, *go home.*

" ' Come unto Me, ye weary,
And I will give you rest.'
O blessed voice of Jesus,
Which comes to hearts opprest ;
It tells of benediction,
Of pardon, grace, and peace,
Of joy that hath no ending,
Of love which cannot cease.

" ' Come unto Me, ye wanderers,
And I will give you light.'
O loving voice of Jesus,
Which comes to cheer the night ;
Our breasts were filled with sadness,
And we had lost our way ;
But He has brought us gladness,
And songs at break of day.

" ' Come unto Me, ye fainting,
And I will give you life.'
O cheering voice of Jesus,
Which comes to aid our strife ;
The foe is stern and eager,
The fight is fierce and long ;
But He has made us mighty,
And stronger than the strong.

" ' And whomsoever cometh,
I will not cast him out.'
O welcome voice of Jesus,
Which drives away our doubt ;
Which calls us very sinners,
Unworthy though we be,
Of love so free and boundless,
To come, dear Lord, to Thee.

SERMON IX.

The Faithful Friend.

S. JOHN VI. 37.

" Him that cometh to Me I will in no wise cast out."

THERE are some words which are equally beautiful in all
languages. The name *Mother*, for instance, in all tongues,
and in all ages, means love, sweetness, gentleness, trust.
In the old Bible days when a Hebrew child murmured
that name by its mother's knee, beneath the shadow of
the vine and fig-tree in Emmanuel's land ; in the warrior
days of ancient Greece or Rome, when the soldier in his
armour stopped to listen to his little one prattling in his
wife's arms ; to-day when we pause to hearken to our
child's first speech, it is always the same ; we hear the
word, which in Hebrew, or Greek, or Latin, in the soft
southern tongue of Italy, or in the sturdy Anglo-Saxon
of our own land, means the same thing—love, sweetness,
trust—*Mother*. There is another such word which is
beautiful in any tongue, and that is the word *Friend*.
I should not care to learn a language which had not that
word ; I should not think this life worth living if I had

not a friend. The hardest, saddest thing, which can be said of a man is " he has no friends." There is something very grand and holy about an earthly friendship ; such a friendship as that of Damon, which made him willing to die for Phintias, or that of Jonathan for David. It is a blessed thought that here in the world we have some one who cares for us, one who will rejoice at our success, and be sorry for our failure. Such a friend is better than thousands of gold and silver, better than houses and lands, for these are valueless if we are without a friend. But earthly friends change. The friends of our childhood, who played with us in the meadows at home, are scattered far and wide. Some are fighting the battle of life in foreign lands, others pass us in the crowd without knowing us. Many are in their graves. The very fields where we played are built over and become a town. Some of the friends who promised to be always faithful to us quarreled about politics, or allowed a little money, or a little land to separate us for ever. Yes, earthly friends change. But the hymn which we sang just now tells us of a Friend who never changes, " with whom is no variableness, neither shadow of turning ; Jesus Christ, the same yesterday, to-day, and for ever." Let us think, then, of Jesus as being our best Friend, *first, because of what He did for us, and is doing for us now.* Some of our earthly friends will do much for us, but who could or would do what Jesus has done ? He did not merely say that He loved

us, He proved it. He became poor for our sakes, that
He might make us rich. He gave up Heaven for us,
and exchanged the good things which eye hath not
seen, nor ear heard, the ministry of angels and the worship
of saints, for a homeless earth. He exchanged the songs
of Heaven for the angry voices of wicked men, the Name
which is above every name for one of reproach, the
unsearchable riches of God for poverty and want. He
was stripped of His garments that we might be clothed
with the white robes of righteousness. He had no place
to lay His Head that we might enter into that rest which
remaineth for the people of God. He was hungry that
we might receive the Bread of Life; He thirsted that He
might give us to drink out of the well of salvation. He
was despised on earth that we might be exalted in
Heaven, He was rejected of men that we might be
accepted of God. He allowed His eyes to be blind-
folded that our eyes might one day see the King in His
beauty. He wore the crown of thorns that we might
wear the crown of glory. O marvellous Friendship for
those who did not love Him, who were even His enemies,
since whilst we were yet sinners, Christ died for us!

And Jesus did all this willingly. The Son of God, who
could have called down legions of angels to help Him,
allowed a few soldiers to kill Him. God, who made all
men, died for the men whom He had made. And *Jesus
is our best Friend, because of what He is doing for us now.*

He dwells with us; Emanuel, God with us. He gives us day by day our daily bread, food for the soul as well as for the body. As He gives bodily bread to strengthen man's heart, so He gives the Bread from Heaven in the Blessed Sacrament to strengthen man's soul. He daily renews in us, by the work of the Holy Spirit, all that sin and temptation have destroyed in us. He is in us as a well of water ever flowing up to refresh us and keep us alive. And besides all this, He is in Heaven ever pleading for us at the right hand of God. Again, Jesus is our Best Friend because He is the *unchanging Friend of all the kinds of people who will love Him.* Jesus is the same yesterday, the yesterday of childhood. Holy Child Jesus is the Friend of little children. The poorest cradle is not too mean for Him who lay in a manger. Jesus, the learner, who when twelve years old was in the Temple hearing, and asking questions, is the Friend of the school-boy, and leads him in the path of wisdom. And Jesus is the same to-day. He is our Friend to-day. The Friend of Lazarus, the Friend of the penitent woman, the Friend of Jairus' dead child, is our Friend to-day. Hear how He calls us according to our several needs—

> " Come unto Me, ye weary,
> And I will give you rest."

Ah ! who among us is not weary sometimes ? Some of us are " weary with the march of life," weary with the battle against temptation, weary with the battle for bread. On the path of some dead hopes and disappointed wishes lie like dead leaves ; and visions of brighter days never to come, fly past us like broken clouds. We look for some one to have pity, and there is no one. Then comes the gentle voice, saying, "Come unto me, ye weary." Most of us are weary of our sins. We are " weary of earth and laden with our sin." We try to climb up to better things, and we fall back so often ; we want to do right, yet evil seems ever present. Then we are forced to cry—" Who will show us any good ? Who will deliver us from the body of this death ?" Then comes the answer—

" 'Come unto Me, ye weary,
And I will give you rest.'
O blessed voice of Jesus,
Which comes to hearts opprest ;
It tells of benediction,
Of pardon, grace, and peace,
Of joy that hath no ending,
Of love which cannot cease."

Some among us are weary of their cross. They want to be saved *from* their cross, like the impenitent thief, instead of *by* the cross, like him who repented. They murmur " it is so hard to bear all this trouble, so hard to give up what I love best, why are these trials laid upon me ?" Then the gentle answer comes, "O weary ones,

O weary hearts, and aching brows, O tired pilgrims
through the wilderness of this world, cast your burden
upon the Lord,"—

> " Come unto Me, ye wanderers,
>   And I will give you light."

Many of us are filled with sadness, and we have lost
our way.   All looks dark and threatening around us.
Egypt and its bondage are behind, the desert and its
dangers before, and we cannot see the lights of home.
Whither shall we direct our steps ; what must we believe
amid the strife of tongues, and the confusion of speech ?
Again, the answer comes—

> " Come unto Me, ye fainting,
>   And I will give you life."

Some of us lie by the wayside of life, wounded ; Satan
has robbed us, and stripped us, and has left us half-dead.
We have fought in the battle of life, and the foe has been
too strong for us.   Our armour is broken, we faint, we
die.   Hearken !   One comes our way.   " Jesus of
Nazareth passeth by." Jesus, the Good Samaritan passeth
by.   He calls to us and says, " Come unto Me, ye
fainting."   He will make us strong, He will give us
new life.

> " O cheering voice of Jesus,
>   Which comes to aid our strife ;

> The foe is stern and eager,
> The fight is fierce and long ;
> But He has made us mighty,
> And stronger than the strong."

But is Jesus *my* Friend ?   Ah ! how many sad, doubting
hearts have asked that question !   In their sorrow they
cry—I have so often offended Him ; I have so frequently
broken His laws ; I have wandered so very far away from
Him ; I have been a prodigal son, and a wandering sheep.
Will He say me nay ?   Hear the precious answer—

> " Whomsoever cometh,
> I will not cast him out."

Jesus waits for you, He longs for you, He cries to you,
" Let Me be your Friend."   All He wants in us is true
sorrow for our past sin, and a hearty desire to do better ;
" since God who made us without ourselves, will not save
us without ourselves."   If there be one who hears me now
whose heart is sad with the sense of sin, and who longs
for better things, let him arise and go to Jesus his Friend.

> " ' And whomsoever cometh,
> I will not cast him out.'
> O welcome voice of Jesus,
> Which drives away our doubt ;
> Which calls us very sinners,
> Unworthy though we be,
> Of love so free and boundless,
> To come, dear Lord, to Thee."

" Abide with me ; fast falls the eventide ;
    The darkness deepens ; Lord, with me abide ;
    When other helpers fail, and comforts flee,
    Help of the helpless, O abide with me.

" Swift to its close ebbs out life's little day;
    Earth's joys grow dim, its glories pass away ;
    Change and decay in all around I see ;
    O Thou who changest not, abide with me.

" I need Thy presence every passing hour ;
    What but Thy grace can foil the tempter's power ?
    Who like Thyself my guide and stay can be ?
    Through cloud and sunshine, Lord, abide with me.

" I fear no foe with Thee at hand to bless ;
    Ills have no weight, and tears no bitterness ;
    Where is death's sting ? where, grave, thy victory ?
    I triumph still, if Thou abide with me.

" Hold Thou Thy Cross before my closing eyes ;
    Shine through the gloom, and point me to the skies ;
    Heaven's morning breaks, and earth's vain shadows flee,
    In life, in death, O Lord, abide with me."

SERMON X.

S. JOHN VI. 17.

" It was now dark, and Jesus was not come to them."

NIGHT is falling on the Lake of Galilee. The disciples are in a boat alone, rowing towards Capernaum. They have just seen the miraculous feeding of five thousand people with a few loaves; and to escape the grateful and excited crowd, Jesus, having sent away His disciples first, has dismissed the multitude, and retired to a mountain alone to pray. Jesus is up on high, where He has drawn near to His Father in Prayer, in the calm peace of one alone with God the Father. The disciples are below on the sea, full of doubt and anxiety. Here we have a type of two classes of people in the world; the one class calm and peaceful because close to God; the other class out in the stormy world, full of doubt and care because Jesus has not yet come to them. Presently a sudden storm, so common on the Lake of Galilee, arises; the wind sweeps across the barren hills which rise on one side of the lake, and rushes down the valleys opening on the water. In a moment the waves are white with foam, the short twilight dies out, and darkness falls suddenly ; and a great wind blows, so that the disciples labour painfully at the oars. Has Jesus forgotten them ? Will He leave them there to perish ? Straining their eyes through the mist and gloom, they see a bright Form in the blackness. It is Jesus walking upon the sea. At first they are afraid because they know not that it is Jesus ; but presently, through the howling of the storm, comes the well-loved voice, saying, "It is I, be not afraid." Then the disciples willingly receive Jesus into the boat, and immediately there is a calm and safety. All which the labour of the disciples could not do is done in a moment, the ship is at the land whither they go. I see in this scene a parable of our lives. Let us think of it in connection with the hymn so familiar to us all— "Abide with me." We who are Christ's disciples are embarked on the troublesome waves of this world, where storms, and trials, and dangers beset us. Some of us are trying to reach the farther shore without God's help, trusting to our own rowing. With such people it is indeed dark, and Jesus has not come to them. Such are the unbeliever, or the worldly man who professes to do without religion. By-and-bye when the sea rises by reason of a great wind that blows, a wind of loss, or temptation, or sorrow, it is no wonder that the waves of the sea rage horribly, and go even over their soul. But even for those who love their Lord, and who are trying to keep His commandments, it is a very troublesome voyage over the sea of life. There are so many currents, so many rocks and quicksands, storms and tempests, that for us a time often comes when we must say, " it is now dark." When that time comes we need to have Jesus with us. We need to see Him walking over the sea of trouble, then all will be well, and we shall reach the shore whither we go. In such dark hours we need to say, as the disciples said to Jesus on a different occasion, " Abide with us, for it is towards evening, and the day is far spent." Look at the hymn—

> " Abide with me, fast falls the eventide ;
> The darkness deepens ; Lord, with me abide ;
> When other helpers fail, and comforts flee,
> Help of the helpless, O abide with me."

There are dark hours in all our lives, when sorrow is hard at hand ; when the prize for which we laboured slips from our grasp, and the hope which we cherished is disappointed ; when poverty and want fall on our home, or illness casts a shadow over our way of life ; and the voice of wife or child is hushed for ever. These are dark times indeed ; how very dark for those to whom Jesus has not yet come, who do not know where to look for Him. In such dark times as these we cry out for light, since what are we all, but as—

> " An infant crying in the night,
> An infant crying for the light,
> And with no language but a cry ?"

Ah ! brethren, we want Jesus with us in these dark hours. We need to feel that " the Lord our God will lighten our darkness; the Lord will light our candle." We need to see Jesus walking on the sea of trouble, and saying to us, " It is I, be not afraid."

> " When other helpers fail and comforts flee,
> Help of the helpless, O abide with me."

For us all the shadows are lengthening.

> " Swift to its close ebbs out life's little day ;
> Earth's joys grow dim, its glories pass away."

For us all the evening-time comes on very fast; every day shows us that the sun of our life is lower, and the shadows longer. With the old people it is evening already. They know that for them very soon "the night cometh when no man can work." How will they take that last journey through the valley of the shadow of death alone? A lonely old age, when we have outlived friends and relations, is sad enough, but how much worse is an old age without God, without light, when " it is now dark, and Jesus has not come to them." O, you who are old, round whom the shadows of night are gathering, let your prayer be to Jesus—

> " Abide with me, fast falls the eventide."

For all of us the time comes when—

> "Earth's joys grow dim, its glories pass away."

A time when all that was sweetest and brightest in life has
lost its savour, when the dim eyes can no more look on the
sunshine, and the deaf ears fail to listen to the music.
As a child grows up it cares nothing for the toys in which
it once delighted. So there comes a time when the
crown to the king, and money to the wealthy, and
pleasure to the frivolous, are like cast-off toys. The days
come when of all these things we say, " I have no pleasure
in them." Change and decay are all around, the great
future is before, and all we need is Jesus to abide with us.

Again, there is a dark time when we fall into temptation, when Satan thrusts sore at us, when " the good that
we would, we do not, and the evil that we would not,
that we do." These dark times of temptation come to
all, to the very best of us. The holiest saints have had
the fiercest temptations. Woe unto us in that hour of
darkness if Jesus be not come to us ; if we have not cried
to Him, " Lord, save us, we perish." When our feet
stick fast in the deep mire, when we are weary of crying,
when there seems no break in the black clouds, then
above all times our prayer should be, " Abide with me,
for it is toward evening."

> " I need Thy presence every passing hour ;
> What but Thy grace can foil the tempter's power?"

If Jesus be with us in the ship in the dark time of sorrow
and temptation, the storm will have lost its power over

us. "Ills have no weight, and tears no bitterness." The storm may still rage, but we shall not be cast away.

But again, a time must come to us all when it is dark; when the shadow of death falls upon us, and we must go forth on that journey where there are no footprints backward. When our strength faileth us, and the light of our eyes is quenched, then it is "toward evening" with us, and then, indeed, we need Jesus to abide with us. Some death scenes are all dark, "it is now dark, and Jesus has not come to them." The man who never knew Jesus in life, seldom finds Him in death. "They die, and make no sign." But those who have been with Jesus on the stormy sea of life, may hope to "find Him on the other side of the sea." If Jesus abides with them, all is well even in death. "Yea, the darkness is no darkness" to them. Those who have Jesus with them have light in their dwellings, both in the hour of death, and in the day of Judgment. There is a beautiful story of a poor working-man, who had had many sorrows and trials, but who loved his Saviour. One night he fell down the shaft of an old forsaken coal-pit, and as he lay crushed and mangled, knowing that he must die, he saw a star shining far above him in the calm sky. And the fancy came to him that it was the very star which guided to our Saviour's home, and thus in that terrible evening time it was light. In course of time he was found, but as they carried him homewards he died; "the star had shown him where to find the God of the poor; and through humility, and sorrow, and forgiveness, he had gone to his Saviour's rest." Men of science tell us that the first thing which a new-born child does is to turn its eyes to the light. And we all know that just before death the dying always crave for light. But the Christian longs for something more than physical light, he looks for the light of God's countenance, for Jesus to abide with him. A famous schoolmaster in the hour of death fancied he was once again in his school-room, and said, "it is growing dark, boys, we must put off the rest till to-morrow." For you and me there will come a time when of our work, and our pleasure, and our life, we shall be forced to say, "we must put off the rest till to-morrow"—the tremendous morrow of eternity. For all at the hour of death there comes physical darkness, but for Christ's people the promise is fulfilled, "in the evening-time it shall be light." To some indeed the light seems to come most clearly at the last evening-time of death. "It did not seem to come to them in the morning of youth, and when the midday of life was past, they cast wistful, almost reproachful petitions to Heaven, and it seemed that there was neither voice nor any that regarded. But in the evening comes an answer, and comes light." Then, though the darkness of death falls, and the winter of sorrow is hard, the dying man can feel the brightness of Paradise in spite of darkened windows and sad faces, like one of whom the poet says,

> " Spite of thick air and closëd doors,
> God told him it was June."

Surely the best sight for our dying eyes is that of Jesus crucified for our sins, and now ever living to make intercession for us. Surely our dying wish should be " We would see Jesus." Surely our dying prayer should be

> " Hold Thou Thy cross before my closing eyes,
> Shine through the gloom and point me to the skies."

Then for us Jesus will say once more " let there be light," and the morning shall break, that morning where no night cometh. Then our lips will yearn to say with the angel, " let me go, for the day breaketh," it is towards evening here, but bright, glorious morning there.

"At even, ere the sun was set,
  The sick, O Lord, around Thee lay
Oh, in what divers pains they met!
  Oh, in what joy they went away.

"Once more 'tis eventide, and we
  Oppressed with various ills draw near ;
What if Thy Form we cannot see?
  We know and feel that Thou art near.

"O Saviour Christ, our woes dispel ;
  For some are sick, and some are sad,
And some have never loved Thee well,
  And some have lost the love they had ;

"And some have found the world is vain,
  Yet from the world they break not free ;
And some have friends who give them pain,
  Yet have not sought a friend in Thee ;

"And none, O Lord, have perfect rest,
  For none are wholly free from sin ;
And they who fain would serve Thee best,
  Are conscious most of wrong within.

"O Saviour Christ, Thou too art man :
  Thou hast been troubled, tempted, tried,
Thy kind but searching glance can scan
  The very wounds that shame would hide.

"Thy touch has still its ancient power ;
  No word from Thee can fruitless fall ;
Hear, in this solemn evening hour,
  And in Thy mercy heal us all."

SERMON XI.

The Healing Touch.

S. MARK I. 32.

" And at even, when the sun did set, they brought unto Him all that were diseased, and them that were possessed with devils."

AGAIN the scene is by the Lake of Galilee, the spot so closely connected with the words and works of Jesus. It is the close of the Sabbath, the first Sabbath of our Lord's public ministry: and He has passed it in Capernaum, " His own city," then a prosperous and beautiful town, overlooking the bright waters of the Lake. The Lake is there to-day, as fresh and fair as when the Apostles' fishing boats sailed there, and Jesus taught the people out of the ship. But of Capernaum nothing remains but a few broken pieces of marble, half buried among thistles and rank grass. The pride and unbelief of Capernaum have had their reward. " Thou, Capernaum, that art exalted unto Heaven, shall be brought down to Hell !"

But on that Sabbath long ago, Capernaum was in all its prosperity and pride. Jesus was staying at the house of S. Peter, where He found the mother of the Apostle's wife ill of a fever, and He healed her. The news spread far and wide through Capernaum, where there must have been many sick and sad folk, as there are in every large town. Scarcely waiting for the Sabbath to end, no sooner does the setting sun tell of evening, than a crowd of people of all classes and ages, seeks Simon's house, bringing with them all that were diseased, and them that were possessed of devils.

> " At even, ere the sun was set,
> The sick, O Lord, around Thee lay—
> Oh, in what divers pains they met !
> Oh, with what joy they went away !"

It must have been a wonderful scene. The fair white town, with its trees and gardens bathed in the colours of sunset : the lake below, calm and beautiful, reflecting every rosy cloud ; and in contrast to all this, the crowd of afflicted people. Blind men were there who had never seen the white town, nor the lake by which they dwelt : lame and paralyzed men who had never done a day's work, and who sadly watched the fishermen launching their boats, and letting down their nets for a draught. Pale, hollow-eyed women were in the crowd, who had spent all their substance on doctors, and were no better, and children with twisted limbs and stammering tongues. There were seen the flushed face and wild eye of fever, the shaking limbs of palsy, and worst of all, the foaming mouths and savage shriek of those possessed by devils. It is no wonder that "the whole multitude sought to touch Him, for there went virtue out of Him and healed them all."

What rejoicing there must have been in the streets of Capernaum that night! How the dumb people, whose tongues were loosed, must have shouted for joy! How the blind, who could say, "whereas I was blind, now I see," must have gazed on the face of Jesus who had healed them, how the lame must have leaped for joy! To those sick folk, condemned so long to darkness and pain and loneliness, that fair scene must have seemed more like Heaven than earth, since, for the sick man restored to health—

> " The meanest flow'ret of the vale,
> The simplest note that swells the gale,
> The common sun, the air, the skies,
> To him are opening Paradise."

Ah! what happy gatherings there must have been in Capernaum homes that night. Mothers clasped their little ones whose once wan cheeks were now rosy with health. The dumb man told his deaf neighbour the story of his cure. Those once possessed with devils knelt to thank God for deliverance. Well, all this happened long ago. Capernaum and its people have long since been called to their account.

But yet there are sick and sorrowful people in the

world, and Jesus yet lives as the Good Physician to heal
them.   There still goes virtue out of Him as of old, and
if we may but touch Him we shall be made whole.

> " Once more 'tis eventide, and we
>   Oppressed with various ills draw near ;
>   What if Thy Form we cannot see ?
>   We know and feel that Thou art here."

Although we cannot look on Jesus as those people did
in Capernaum, yet we are certain that He is amongst us,
for He has said, " Wherever two or three are gathered
together in my name, there am I in the midst of them."
And what are we all but a crowd of sick people who need
to touch Jesus ?

> " O Saviour, Christ, our woes dispel,
>   For some are sick, and some are sad,
>   And some have never loved Thee well,
>   And some have lost the love they had.

> " And some have found the world is vain,
>   Yet from the world they break not free ;
>   And some have friends who give them pain,
>   Yet have not sought a friend in Thee."

I think there are a great many *blind people* among us ;
so blind that they cannot see their own sins.   The man
who commits sin with his eyes open, knowing it to be
wrong, knowing what God says about it, and yet
deliberately does it ; the man who is not strictly honest
in business and in his work, who is not strictly truthful in

dealing with others, who confesses that what he does is wrong, and yet does it, that man is blind.

The people who sin against purity, who are not ashamed to do what decent people are ashamed to talk of, who when reproved try to laugh the matter off, who try to pretend that it is a sin of little consequence : these people are blind.

Yes, and so are all those who think more of this life than of the life eternal; and what a crowd of such blind folk there is among us. These are very quick-sighted in worldly affairs, very sharp men of business, very keen at making a bargain. They are very careful about the title deeds of their estate, but careless of their inheritance in Heaven. They are very accurate in keeping their business accounts, they know what they owe to men, but they forget what they owe God. They are punctual about seed-time and harvest, but negligent of the seed-time of their life, and the great harvest at the end of the world. They are very much in earnest about getting up in this world, but quite indifferent about getting up so high as Heaven. They are particular about wearing a respectable suit of clothes, but careless about the heart which it covers. I say these people are blind. If I were to hold a crown of gold and purse of money over a blind man's head, he would take no heed, he would go on groping in the dark as before, because he is blind. So when God holds the crown of Life Eternal, and the treasure of Heaven, over

G

a worldly man's head, he goes on groping in the earth, and takes no heed, because he is blind.

Next, I think, there are a *great many lame people among us.* There are spiritual cripples as well as physical cripples. These are the people who will walk in any way rather than the right way; who instead of keeping straight in the path of holiness, will go crooked into the foul bye-paths of evil. Who instead of following the directions of Christ's Gospel, go their own way, and lose themselves. Who prefer the slippery paths of deceit and hypocrisy, to the ways of God's laws, and the works of His commandments. These are the people who will walk almost any distance for work or pleasure, but are always too tired to come to Church: who never find their fields too wide, or their place of business too distant, but always complain of the long journey to Church; forgetting that even if the way be long, an angel counts their footsteps. Then there are those who walk straight for a little while; who after their Confirmation come to the Sacrament of the Altar for a time, and then fall away and get on the wrong road; these are the people whom I call spiritual cripples.

I think, too, there are a great many *deaf and dumb people among us.* God speaks to them in Church by the message of the Gospel, and they take no heed; they go out of Church, and straightway fall into sin. God speaks to them by some great good which He sends them; they receive the blessing but cannot hear God's voice. He speaks to them by some great loss or sorrow, and they murmur at the trouble, but cannot hear God speaking to them. These are the deaf people. Then there are the dumb people, who say anything but their prayers: who never thank God for the blessings of everyday life; who rise up in the morning, and lie down at night, and never ask God to take care of them. These are the people who in Church never utter a word of praise or prayer; who out of Church never speak a word of help or warning to a neighbour. These are the dumb people.

I think, too, that there are a *great many people among us who are possessed with devils.* There are tens of thousands of people possessed with the devil of drunkenness, exceeding fierce, so that no man can bind them; and thus they become murderers, and wife-beaters, and madmen. There are tens of thousands of people possessed with the devil of lust and impurity, who bring ruin upon innocent homes, and drive their victims to disgrace and death. You can scarcely open a newspaper without seeing how commonly men are possessed with devils of this kind. Many, again, are possessed with the devil of unbelief, making them blaspheme the holy name of God. Others are possessed with the devils of greed and worldliness, driving them to give up all they have, time, and strength, and mind, and soul, to making money. Then, too, there are the devils of bad temper, bad language, discontent,

and many others, of which the time would fail me to
speak.   And even those among us who cannot be said to
be blind, or lame, or dumb, or possessed of devils, and
who are trying to do God's will, these know, none better
than they, how often they are sick with some sin or other,
since—

> " None, O Lord, have perfect rest,
>   For none are wholly free from sin ;
>   And they who fain would serve Thee best,
>   Are conscious most of wrong within."

What then must we all do to be healed from sickness,
and to be strengthened to bear our sorrows ?   Just what
those people did of old at Capernaum, we must draw near
and *touch Jesus*.   We read in the Gospel of a woman
who had tried all kinds of doctors, and spent all her
money upon them, and was no better.   At last she came
to Jesus.   She struggled through the crowd, she came
near, and touched the Lord.   And immediately she was
healed.   Some of you perhaps have been trying other
doctors, and other cures.   One has tried carelessness and
indifference, and has said, " It does not matter what I
do."   Another has tried pride, and has said, " I don't
want to be interfered with."   Another has tried hopeless-
ness, and has cried, " Where is the use of trying, I shall
never be better ?"   Some have tried unbelief.   Ah !
brethren, these are not the doctors to cure you.   Do not
waste your time and substance upon them.   Draw near to
Jesus, and touch Him : struggle through the crowd of

obstacles which stands between you and your Saviour. Perhaps your friends stand between you and Jesus, since,

" Some have friends who give them pain,
Yet have not sought a friend in Thee."

Perhaps it is your work, or your home cares and worries, which come between you and Christ. Struggle through the crowd, whatever it is. Do not rest till you can get close to Jesus, and touch Him. You can do this. Although He no longer stands in bodily form in our midst, yet He has left means by which we may draw near to Him, and touch Him. When we pray earnestly, we draw near and touch Jesus with the outstretched hand of prayer. When a little child, sick with the sin of Adam, comes to Holy Baptism, he draws near and touches Jesus. When you draw near to the Altar of the Blessed Sacrament, there indeed you draw near and touch Jesus. He comes to you veiled in the Sacrament under the form of Bread and Wine; as of old, He came under the humble form of one whom they called the Carpenter's Son ; and then indeed you touch Him with the hands of faith, and receive Him into your heart, and are made whole. Draw near to Him now, all ye who are weary and heavy laden, sad with sorrow, or sick with sin, draw near and touch your Lord in earnest prayer, and let that prayer be now—

" Thy touch has still its ancient power;
No Word from Thee can fruitless fall ;
Hear, in this solemn evening hour,
And in Thy mercy heal us all."

" Holy off'rings, rich and rare,
   Offerings of praise and prayer,
   Purer life, and purpose high,
   Clasped hands, uplifted eye,
   Lowly acts of adoration,
   To the God of our Salvation,—
   On His altar laid we leave them,
   Christ, present them ! God, receive them !

" Promises in sorrow made,
   Left, alas ! too long unpaid ;
   Fervent wishes, earnest thought,
   Never into action wrought—
   Long withheld, we now restore them,
   On Thy holy Altar pour them :
   There in trembling faith to leave them,
   Christ, present them ! God, receive them !"

Holy Offerings.

" The Lord . . . remember all Thy offerings."

" WHAT shall I render unto the Lord for all His benefits towards Me ?" There are people who will say that we can give nothing to God who giveth all; but I do not think they speak the truth. These are the selfish folk who really mean, even if they do not say so, "get all you can from God, God wants no return." Now the Bible says just the opposite. The Bible says, " present your bodies a living sacrifice, holy, acceptable unto God." The people who talk about "the finished work of Christ," and who say that He has done all, and that therefore there is nothing for us to do, forget that there are two parts in the scheme of salvation. Jesus has indeed done His part, but He bids us do certain things also ; He not only came on earth to die for our sins, and to rise again for our justification ; He came also to give us an example, that we might follow the steps of His most holy life, " mortifying our evil and corrupt affections, and daily proceeding in all virtue and godliness of living." And, believe me, this is no very easy matter. There is a line in a hymn which I once read, which says, " cast your deadly doing down." Now nothing can be more foolish than to accept this kind of teaching. If you met two men on the road going to a certain city, and the one man were to say to you, " I have faith that I shall get to my journey's end," and then sat down by the roadside ; and if the other were to say, " I have faith also that God will bring me to my journey's end, but I have also strong legs which God has given me, and I mean to use them ;" I think you would believe in the man who added to his faith a manly determination to do what was required of him. I lately met with a printed paper in which the doctrine of doing nothing was so plainly set forth, that I determined to try and show its falseness. Let me read it to you side by side with the hymn which forms the subject of this sermon. The printed paper of which I spoke, and which exactly declares the doctrine taught from many a pulpit and platform, begins in this way—

" Nothing to pay ?—no, not a whit !
Nothing to *do* ?—no, not a bit !
All that was needed to do or to pay,
Jesus has done in His own blessed way.

" Nothing to *do* ?—no, not a stroke !
Gone is the captor, gone is the yoke,
Jesus at Calvary, severed the chain,
And none can imprison His freemen again.

" Nothing to *fear* ?—no, not a jot ;
Nothing unclean ?—no, not a spot :
Christ is my peace, and I've nothing at stake,
Satan can neither harass nor shake."

Now I would not quote such lines as these did I know how many people are deceived by what they teach. Let us examine the statements here made. We have nothing to *pay*. But, brethren, would it not be base ingratitude if someone had been good and kind to you in trouble, and you had not tried to make some return, however small? Well then, " how much owest thou unto my Lord ?" Do you remember what the Lord Jesus paid for us? Have we nothing to pay, or to give to Him ? You will answer that you have nothing good enough to give to Him. But you have, you can give Him what He asks for, your heart, your love. And, remember, that love is shown in deeds, not in words. It is very easy to *say*, " I love God;" Orpah kissed Naomi, and said that she loved her, but Ruth clave unto her. There is the difference between talking and doing. Many people who say that they love the Lord Jesus Christ, forget those words of His, " If ye love Me, keep My commandments."

How then can we show our love to God, what offerings
can we present to Him ?   Let the hymn tell us—

> "Holy off'rings, rich and rare,
> Offerings of praise and prayer,
> Purer life, and purpose high,
> Clasped hands, uplifted eye,
> Lowly acts of adoration,
> To the God of our salvation,—
> On His altar laid we leave them,
> Christ present them ! God receive them!

In a word, one of the holiest offerings which we can
give to God is *worship*, and it is to offer this worship that
we come to Church.   Many mistakes are made about
Church-going.   One tells us that he goes to Church
because he likes it, he has always been brought up to the
Church.   Another goes because he wants to get good;
another from less worthy motives.   But these are none
of them the true reason why we should go to God's
Temple.   We should go there to make an holy offering
of praise and thanksgiving, an offering of worship.   The
common notion about Church-going springs from sheer
selfishness; people are for ever asking, "what do I
need from God, what good shall I get from going to
Church; what advantage is it to me to listen to a dull
preacher; how can I possibly endure that kind of service?"   This is all selfishness.   It is not a question of
what we want, or like, or desire ; it is not a question of

preferring one preacher to another, or one kind of service to another; the question is—what is my duty towards God, how can I best honour Him who hath done all for me; what reward shall I give unto the Lord for all the benefits which He hath done unto me? Why do we find it so difficult to get people to Church? Why do the hours of service always seem so much longer than any other to certain people? Why does a little bad weather invariably prevent these persons from attending Church, though it never deters them from a place of amusement? The reason is simply this—they have not learnt that they owe something to God, that there *is* "something to pay," and that that something is an holy offering of praise and thanksgiving, and that if this be neglected, God is defrauded.   This is what we can offer to Jesus—

> " Homage of each humble heart,
>   Ere we from Thy house depart,
>   Worship fervent, deep and high,
>   Adoration, ecstasy ;
>   All that childlike love can render,
>   Of devotion true and tender—
>   On Thine Altar laid we leave them ;
>   Christ, present them ! God receive them !"

Above all, we offer an holy offering of praise in the highest act of worship, in the celebration of the Blessed Sacrament of the Altar.   Many people misunderstand this.   They stay away from the Altar and excuse them-

selves by saying " I am not good enough to come ;" or
" I should not get any good if I did come." But this is
not merely a question of getting good, it is rather one of
giving praise in worship and honour to Jesus Christ. He
gives you pardon, peace, strength, in a word, Himself.
But you have to give Him something. You should come
to adore your Saviour, present there in the Sacrament ;
you should draw near to Him who was once forsaken of
all, of whom it was said once, and might be truly said
now, " He is despised, and rejected of men." In the
service of Holy Communion we take part with the saints
and angels in Heaven in worshipping God. Remember
the meaning of those words, " Therefore with angels and
archangels, and all the company of Heaven, we laud and
magnify Thy glorious name, evermore praising Thee, and
saying, Holy, Holy, Holy, Lord God of hosts, heaven
and earth are full of Thy glory; glory be to Thee, O
Lord most high."

Is there, then, nothing to pay ? Oh ! yes, a life of
devotion, a life of thanksgiving ; there is everything to
pay, even the best we have. " I will pay my vows now
in the presence of all His people," says holy David, and
yet there are some who tell us " there is nothing to pay."

Thus far we have seen that we can show our love to
God by giving Him the offering of a holy worship. {Again,
we can make an offering to God by giving alms to His
Church. God gives us all we have, our money, and our

means of making money ; and we are bound to dedicate, to consecrate a part of what we have to Him. Now people are often mistaken about almsgiving. I have known a man to refuse to give to the offertory because he did not like the clergyman ; and I have known another man who would not give because he did not like the way in which the alms were collected. But the reason for this is easy to be understood ; people are thinking about *themselves* instead of God. There are some people who imagine that when they give to the offertory they are paying for a seat in Church. Others give only when coming to the Holy Communion ; and very many give at all times the very least that they can. All these persons have failed to understand that almsgiving in Church is not a favour conferred by them, but a privilege and a duty, to neglect which is to commit sin. When we give to the Church we give to Christ, since the Charch is Christ's Body, and He has said, " Inasmuch that ye have done it unto the least of these, My brethren, ye have done it unto Me." But remember, brethren, the spirit in which you give alms. " The Lord loveth a cheerful giver ;" the offering which is unwillingly and grudgingly given cannot be called an holy offering, nor is it acceptable to God. I have heard of a stingy man who, though well off, always gave a penny to the offertory. One day, by mistake, he gave a shilling. " Well, I shall get credit for the shilling at all events," said he to a friend. " No,"

answered his friend, "you will only get credit for the
penny." There is an old story of a saint who used every
night to wash the feet of twelve beggars. One night a
thirteenth appeared with the twelve, a stranger to all.
The saint asked the stranger who He was, and whence
He came, and the answer was, "Inasmuch as you have
done it unto the least of these, My brethren, you have
done it unto Me;" and then he knew it was the Lord.
How many are there among us who spend their money
freely on a new dress, or a passing pleasure, and yet
grudge the smallest offering to God ! And why? Because
they love *themselves* better than the Lord Jesus Christ.

Again, this false teaching goes on to tells us that there
is nothing *to do*, and nothing *to fear*. What do you think
yourselves? You know that it is written, "without holiness no man can see the Lord." Now, do you think
that you have nothing to do? Do you find it very easy
to lead good lives; to keep God's commandments, to
keep yourselves pure, and gentle, and patient, and for-
giving? Do you find nothing to do in resisting temptation, in keeping under your temper, in checking bad
thoughts? If there is nothing for us to do, S. Paul must
be wrong when he says, "work out your own salvation
with fear and trembling;" and S. Peter must be mistaken
when he bids us "be sober, be vigilant, because your
adversary the devil, as a roaring lion, walketh about,
seeking whom he may devour; whom resist, steadfast in

the faith." If there is nothing for us to do, why does our Lord command us "to watch and pray, lest we enter into temptation?" But, some one will say, all that we can do will not save us. That is quite true. But, as said a saint of old, "God who made us without ourselves, will not save us without ourselves." Jesus has done His part, but He nowhere tells you that you have nothing to do. He died for your sins, and rose again for your justification; He promises you salvation, if you do your part. There is this condition attached. Often when people say, "I belong to Jesus, I am safe," they are simply deceiving themselves. Some of the most atrocious criminals have talked in this way. "By their fruits ye shall know them." If you really do love the Lord Jesus Christ, you will try to obey Him. Jesus died for all, yet all are not saved. He separates the sheep from the goats, the chaff from the wheat, the false coin from the true. Do not let us talk about our having nothing to do, or to pay, or to fear, but rather let us try to devote all we have to God, to pay the devotion of a life-time to Him, " to do all, looking unto Jesus." And do you ask, "*what* must I do?" I answer, repent you truly or your sins past. Offer your repentance as an offering to God, it will be precious in His eyes.

> " Promises in sorrow made,
> Left, alas ! too long unpaid ;
> Fervent wishes, earnest thought,
> Never into action wrought— ·

> Long withheld, we now restore them,
> On Thy holy Altar pour them :
> There in trembling faith to leave them,
> Christ, present them ! God, receive them !"

There is yet another offering which we can give to God, the sacrifice of self. Every act of self-denial, every pleasure abandoned for the sake of others, will be accepted by Him who gave up all for us.

> "Pleasant food, and garb of pride,
> Put for conscience sake aside,
> Lawful luxury foregone
> To relieve some little one
> Loved of Christ, by Him befriended,
> And for His dear love attended—
> On Thine Altar laid we leave them :
> Christ, present them ! God, receive them !"

H

" Onward, Christian soldiers,
   Marching as to war,
   With the Cross of Jesus
   Going on before.
   Christ, the Royal Master,
   Leads against the foe ;
   Forward into battle,
   See His banners go.

" At the sign of triumph
   Satan's host doth flee ;
   On then, Christian soldiers,
   On to victory.
   Hell's foundations quiver
   At the shout of praise ;
   Brothers, lift your voices,
   Loud your anthems raise.

" Like a mighty army
   Moves the Church of God ;
   Brothers, we are treading
   Where the saints have trod ;
   We are not divided,
   All one body we,
   One in hope and doctrine,
   One in charity.

" Crowns and thrones may perish,
   Kingdoms rise and wane,
   But the Church of Jesus
   Constant will remain ;
   Gates of Hell can never
   'Gainst that Church prevail ;
   We have Christ's own promise,
   And that cannot fail.

" Onward then, ye people,
   Join our happy throng,
   Blend with ours your voices
   In the triumph song ;
   Glory, laud and honour
   Unto Christ the King,
   This through endless ages
   Men and angels sing."

SERMON XIII.

The Onward March.

DEUTERONOMY XXXI. 7, 8.

" Be strong and of a good courage,—and the Lord, He it is that doth go before Thee."

So spoke Moses to God's Church of old as they came near to Jordan, and the Promised Land. Dangers and trials were before them, and a path by which they had not travelled as yet, but before them also was the prize, and longed-for rest in Sion. So Moses bid the people to do their part ; as once before by the Red Sea shore they had been told to go forward, so now they were bidden to be strong and of a good courage, for the Lord Himself would go before them. "Speak to the children of Israel, that they go forward ;" "Onward, Christian soldiers ;" such are the watchwords of the Church of Christ. For the Church as a body, and for each of us, its individual members, there must be progress, a going forward, a growth in grace and holiness. For us, as

for Israel of old, there is a journey, a warfare, and a
reward; and for us, as for them, there is the assurance
that the Lord our God goes before us. I once visited
an outward bound ship lying in the Thames, and noticed
her name, which was very striking; it was " Forward Ho !"
I remember that I told the crew that there was the motto
for every Christian, afloat or ashore—Forward Ho ! As
that ship went ever forward through new dangers and
obstacles, through swelling waves and gathering storms,
till she reached the port whither she was bound, so must
our course be, ever forward ho, over the waves of this
troublesome world, through storms of affliction and
temptation, till we enter the haven where we would be.

 We see that the command "go forward" has been
obeyed by the Church at large. There has ever been growth
and advancement. From the one family of Abraham
grew the whole Jewish Church. From the few faithful
people met in the upper room after the Ascension, grew
the whole Christian Church. And that Church is constantly advancing, marching onward to do battle with
ignorance, and wickedness, and heresy, and schism. But
to each one of us, as individual members of the Church,
the command is given to go forward. From the day
when the seed of grace is sown in our hearts at Baptism,
we must go forward and onward, till we reach the river of
death, and pass to Jesus in the better land, where our
progress will not cease, but go on to such good things as

the world cannot give. If we would succeed in the battle of life we must be able to say—

> " Let us go forth, and resolutely dare,
> With sweat of brow, to toil our little day."

And so, believe me, brethren, as Christian men, if we want to succeed, if we want to be holy, if we want to reach Heaven, we must *go forward*, fighting, praying, watching, and waiting, but never idle, never looking back. "God helps those who help themselves." This is no less true in religious life than in our worldly business. He is a coward who expects God to do for him the work which he ought to do for himself. He is shrinking from his duty. God will do for us what we cannot do for ourselves, but we must do our part. It has been said of some of the good old English navigators, who sailed to the new world, that they were " indomitable, God-fearing men, whose life was one great liturgy." But they did something more than pray. They worked, and fought their way through dangers and difficulties, calling on God to help them, and doing their best for themselves.

> " In daily toil, in deadly fight,
> God's chosen found their time to pray;
> And still He loves the brave and strong,
> Who scorn to starve, and strive with wrong,
> To mend it, if they may."

So should it be with us. Knowing that the Lord is on

our side, knowing that He it is that does go before us,
our watchword should be—

> " Onward, Christian soldiers,
>   Marching as to war,
>   With the Cross of Jesus
>   Going on before."

Each one of us, from the little child to the grey-haired
veteran, has a battle to fight with the evil in him, and
around him. And in this warfare he must go forward.
There must be progress in the spiritual life of each
individual soul. As the Church, as a whole, advances
daily in its victorious march against sin and error, so
each one of us ought to go forward and upward daily in
our spiritual life. Do not be satisfied because you won
a victory yesterday. Satan has many reserve forces to
bring against you. Once, in the midst of a battle, an
officer rode up to Sir Charles Napier, and said, " Sir, we
have taken a standard." The general made no reply,
but continued talking to one of his staff. "Sir,"
repeated the messenger, "we have taken a standard."
"Then take another," was the brief answer. If, by God's
grace, you overcame some fault yesterday, and resisted
some temptation, strive to gain another victory to-day—
go forward. It is perseverance, not enthusiasm, which
wins a battle in the field; and in the Christian warfare
he who strives daily to get nearer to God, and farther
from self; who tries daily to go forward, will win the

battle; not the sudden convert who expects to spring at one bound into the front rank of God's saints. But in our onward march we not only have a Leader whom we trust, but we have companions, good and faithful men and women to the right and to the left of us, before us, and behind. It is a great help in an earthly battle for a soldier to feel that he has true and brave comrades marching with him, shoulder to shoulder. So that if he falls, another will be ready to take his place; if he is wounded, kindly hands will be ready to carry him out of the press; if he does well, hearty voices will be ready to cheer him. So we Christian soldiers know that we form one great army, the Church of Christ, enlisted in the same way, bound by the same rules, fed by the same Sacramental food, fighting the same battle, looking for the same reward.

> " We are not divided,
> All one body we,
> One in hope and doctrine,
> One in Charity."

Some of our brethren have finished their earthly march and warfare, they have fought the good fight, and have kept the faith; and these from their resting places pray for us who are still enduring the burden and heat of the day. Others are with us in the battle, bound to us by one faith, one hope of our calling, one Baptism; and their prayers, their sympathy, help us to fight, and " to keep rank." But in our march and our warfare we have something else to do besides fighting. We must *watch.* Perhaps the hardest part of a soldier's duty is that of keeping watch at an outpost. In the thick of the battle, in the rush of a headlong charge, all is excitement and enthusiasm; but the lonely watch for an enemy, who may come at any moment, or not at all, this is a hard task. So with us, some of us do not often meet with fierce temptations to sin; the hosts of Satan do not charge upon us, as it were. But in our daily lives we have to keep watch over word, and thought and temper; and this is indeed hard work. There are people whose lives are full of worry, who have to watch lest they lose faith, or become fretful, or unkind. There are husbands with small means and extravagant wives; and hard-working wives with reckless husbands. There are sickly people who have never felt strong, and who cannot afford the comforts and luxuries which they require. There are those who have seen their fondest hopes blighted, and their cherished plans frustrated; people whose house is left unto them desolate; for such as these the battle is very hard, just because it is one of watching, and waiting, and patiently enduring, since it is

> " Easier to smite with Peter's sword,
>   Than watch one hour in humbling prayer;
>   Life's "great things," like the Syrian lord,
>   Our hearts can do and dare."

There is yet another thought to encourage us in our onward march. Our path is a well-worn path, trodden by thousands before us; our battle field is the scene of countless victories.

> " Brothers ye are treading
> Where the saints have trod."

If an army is called on to fight on the scene of some former victory, we can imagine how eagerly the young soldiers would listen to the story of their fathers' deeds on that same field. How keenly would they mark the spot where one died to save the colours, or where the devoted regiment fought its way through overwhelming numbers to victory. And looking on these scenes, the soldiers of to-day would determine to do or die as bravely as those who fought before them. Well, my brothers, the path you tread has been trodden by such an one as Paul the aged. In the battle in which you fight have fought such soldiers of the Cross as S. Peter and S. John. The path which you tread has often been wet with the tears of saints and martyrs, young men and maidens, old men and children, who have travelled the same way before you. But above all, the Lord Jesus has trodden that path before you, and fought the same bitter battle, and gotten the victory. It is He who says to all of us, "Onward, Christian soldiers." And as we obey His voice, and go forward, we must expect to go forward into *sorrow.* When the path seems very hard to travel on, look for the foot-prints of Jesus who travelled that way before you. See how the Blood of the Saviour marks all the road, and remember that you are not alone in your sorrow. Jesus, the Man of Sorrows, the Lord your God, He it is that doth go before you.

And in your onward march you must expect to go forward into temptation and trial. But take courage, look at the thorny path of trial, and see there the shadows of the wilderness, and of Gethsemane, the shadows of the fasting and temptation, and let your cry be "By Thy fasting and temptation, by Thine agony and bloody sweat, good Lord, deliver us." And as you go onward you must expect to meet with bereavement. You cannot go far on your journey without finding a Cross, your Cross. Then think of that other Cross on Calvary, and remember that Jesus has been here, in this your bitter agony, before you. If your Cross be to see some one very dear to you taken away, try to see Jesus leading that loved one by the hand to the Better Land, and to feel as did one who says—

> " And tho' my heart was breaking,
>   I strove my will to bow,
>   For I saw His Hands were piercèd,
>   And thorns had torn His brow."

Once again, I bid you go " Onward, Christian soldiers,"

remembering that in all your battles, in all your journey-ings, in all your trials and temptations, Jesus is with you. And when at the last you come to the end of your earthly journey, and the river of death must be crossed, remember that Jesus has passed that way before you, and that His Hand is ready to guide you to the shore.

"Jesu, Lover of my soul,
  Let me to Thy Bosom fly,
  While the gathering waters roll,
  While the tempest still is high :
  Hide me, O my Saviour, hide,
  Till the storm of life be past ;
  Safe into the haven guide,
  O receive my soul at last.

"Other refuge have I none ;
  Hangs my helpless soul on Thee ;
  Leave, ah ! leave me not alone,
  Still support and comfort me.
  All my trust on Thee is stayed,
  All my help from Thee I bring ;
  Cover my defenceless head
  With the shadow of Thy wing.

"Plenteous grace with Thee is found,
  Grace to cleanse from every sin ;
  Let the healing streams abound,
  Make and keep me pure within ;
  Thou of Life the Fountain art ;
  Freely let me take of Thee ;
  Spring Thou up within my heart,
  Rise to all eternity."

SERMON XIV.

The Safe Refuge.

" I will say of the Lord, He is my refuge and my fortress."

To the Jew of old human life was a sacred thing, as
being the gift of God. If, therefore, a man slew his
neighbour, even by accident, his own life must pay the
forfeit. The nearest kinsman of the dead became the
Avenger of blood, and was bound to slay the slayer unless
he could escape. For him who had shed blood innocently
there was a means of escape, for the murderer there was
none. He who had shed blood accidentally might escape
to one of the six Cities of Refuge, where he might
remain till the death of the High Priest. These Cities
were placed on either side of the river Jordan, three on
each side. The roads leading to them were always kept
in good repair, and there were direction posts placed at
intervals to point out the way, and bearing the word—
Refuge. Often a pale, weary fugitive was seen hurrying
towards one of these Cities of Refuge ; casting anxious

looks behind, and fancying in every sound the footstep of the Avenger of blood. We can picture such an one reaching the place of safety, and crying, " Thank God! I am safe at last."

Well, as for the Jew of old, so for us to-day, unless we flee to our City of Refuge we are all dead men. What then have we to fly from, and what is our City of Refuge ? First, we need to fly from *the sins and temptations of the world*. Everywhere around in God's beautiful world we find man's sin. As you will see a once fair and sparkling stream poisoned and rendered foul by the impurities of some great city, and the fair face of nature rendered hideous ; so in the world of men you will find human nature rendered hideous by sin. I look at a great city. I see there prosperity, wealth, commercial enterprise, busy men and women, and I know that the place is reeking with sin. I know that here men lie and cheat and over-reach each other. I know that here men curse and blaspheme the name of God ; that there are many who are drunken, many who are unclean, many who are mean, and selfish, and cruel. I look at a country village. I see a fair spot, and I think how simple, and pure, and innocent must be the lives of the people. And yet I know that discontent and hatred flourish here among the flowers, and that many of the people are in their habits less noble than the beasts which perish. From such lives we have need to flee away and escape.

Again, we need to escape from *the sinful feelings and desires of our own hearts.* What do I hear you say? Your hearts are not so bad? Let us hear what God says in the Bible about our hearts: " The heart of man is deceitful above all things, and desperately wicked ;" " Man looketh on the outward appearance, but the Lord looketh on the heart." What does God, "to whom all hearts be open, all desires known, and from whom no secrets are hid," see in our hearts? Is there no selfishness, no pride, no coldness there? Are there no thoughts and desires which we keep secret from men, but which God knows all about? From these things we have need to escape.

And we have need to escape *from the troubles and sorrows of life.* " Man is born to trouble as the sparks fly upward." This life has been wet with tears ever since Adam shed the first tears over a lost Paradise. From the day when Adam mourned over the grave of Abel, the grave-digger has never been without employment. In all ranks of life we find sorrow, and anxiety, and care, and sickness, and death. And we need to flee from these for comfort. Where, then is our City of Refuge?

Let the hymn tell us :—

> " Jesu, Lover of my soul,
> Let me to Thy bosom fly,
> While the gathering waters roll,
> While the tempest still is high :

Hide me, O my Saviour, hide,
Till the storm of life be past ;
Safe into the haven guide,
O receive my soul at last."

Yes, Jesus Christ is "a place to hide us in," He is our
City of Refuge, since "there is none other Name under
Heaven given among men whereby we must he saved."
If the Jew of old had sought any other city instead of one
of the six appointed Cities of Refuge, the Avenger of
blood would have slain him.   The fugitive did not go to
Jerusalem, or to Bethlehem, or to some other place of his
own choosing, he might only find refuge in the place
assigned for him.   So with us, we may not choose a City
of Refuge for ourselves.   There are not even six cities
for us to select from : for us there is only one place of
safety—

"Other refuge have I none,
Hangs my helpless soul on Thee ;"

and we must seek for Jesus, our Refuge, not in places of
man's devising, not among the strife of sects, and the
clamour of different doctrines, but in the place where He
has chosen to put His Name there, His Holy Church,
the same throughout the world.   There we are safe in the
Ark, as was Noah when the Lord had shut him in.   The
unbelieving world laughed at Noah's faith, "what time
the Ark was a building."   They thought the flood would
not come upon them, or that they might escape in an Ark

of their own. So it is with many people now. They will
not come into the ark of Christ's Church; they think the
flood of sin and sorrow will not touch them; or if it does,
they will trust to an Ark of their own—some sect of their
own choosing, some form of religion of their own inven-
tion. But now, as of old, there is but one Ark of safety
from the flood, one appointed place of refuge from the
enemy and Avenger. With Jesus we are safe from sin.
The City of Refuge is one against which the gates of Hell
cannot prevail. The strongest earthly fortresses have
fallen. Even the Rock of Gibraltar has been taken. But
our fortress is the Body of Christ, and Satan, the enemy,
cannot harm it. In our City of Refuge we find peace,
and joy, and rest: no matter how fierce the tempest
outside, no matter how the heathen furiously rage.
There is a legend of the Jews that the dove, sent forth by
Noah from the Ark, plucked the olive leaf, with which she
returned, in the garden of Eden, which was too loftily
situated to be reached by the flood. So we in the Ark
of Christ's Church receive the olive leaf of peace and
joy, brought to us from Paradise by the Heavenly Dove,
the Holy Ghost, the Comforter. I do not tell you that
sin does not come to us in the Church; but we know that
there we may find a place of repentance, a place of absolution, a place of pardon, since Jesus "is faithful and
just to forgive us our sins, and to cleanse us from all un-
righteousness." I do not tell you that we shall never be

I

tempted, never feel weak in our City of Refuge. But I do tell you, that there we can receive the Bread of Life, which will strengthen our souls to resist temptation ; that there the streams of Blood and Water flow from the wounded side of Jesus, in the Sacraments, to give us all we need.

> " Plenteous grace with Thee is found,
> Grace to cleanse from every sin;
> Let the healing streams abound,
> Make and keep me pure within."

If the Jew wandered outside the City of Refuge he was in danger of death. So if we stay outside our Refuge, or having entered, wander away into evil courses, or places of refuge of our own choosing, then we shall prove the truth of the promise, " The soul that sinneth it shall die." " How then shall we escape if we neglect so great salvation ?"

My brethren, there are some among us who are still surrounded with the flood of sin, and the waves of a troublesome world, and have not yet come into the Ark. They have looked at the Ark perhaps with longing eyes, they have sighed for peace and safety there, yet have not obeyed the command, " Come thou and all Thy house into the Ark."

There are some among us who have broken God's law, and the Avenger is pursuing after them ; for every sin brings its punishment ; the Avenger may be slow of foot, but he comes on surely.

If there be one who hears me now who feels the weight of sin heavy on him ; who has been seeking rest and finding none ; fleeing for refuge where no refuge was ; I say to him, "escape for thy life," and escape *now*. The Bible points to the way, saying, " Refuge, Refuge." Come to the Lord Jesus through the door of repentance, saying—

> " ' Weary of earth, and laden with my sin,"

> " Foul, I to the the Fountain fly,
> Wash me, Saviour, or I die."

You will have no peace till you have passed through the way of repentance, and have found pardon, and a place of Refuge.

And, again, Jesus is our Refuge from *trouble.* Some of the sorrows of this life are very bitter. It is false to say we must not be sorry, and shed no tear. To be indifferent does not mean to be resigned. To steel our heart against sorrow is not to be like that Jesus who wept for Lazarus. It *is* very hard to see our wife or child fade as the grass. It *is* hard to miss the patter of baby feet, and the song of baby lips. It *is* hard to see the bread-winner brought home crushed and dead, or to find the bank broken, or the business ruined. But the greater the sorrow the greater our need of comfort. In times of severe affliction the world cannot comfort us. People mean to be kind and sympathetic, but they are thinking of their own affairs. They are glad that misfortune has not fallen upon them, that their dear ones are well, or their money safe. Jesus, the Man of Sorrows, alone has a heart great enough for all the troubles of His people. The only way to bear our cross is to seek the help of Him who bore His Cross to Calvary. The only refuge in time of trouble is with Him who is "our strong rock and our castle."

O widowed mother, remember her of Nain! O bereaved sisters, think of the sisters of Bethany! O mourning parents, recall the daughter of Jairus! O struggling people, tried and troubled in one way or another, fly to the City of Refuge, go to Him who says to you, "Come unto me all ye that travail, and are heavy laden, and I will give you rest."

" I am not worthy, Holy Lord,
   That Thou should'st come to me ;
   Speak but the Word ; one gracious Word
   Can set the sinner free.

" I am not worthy ; cold and bare
   The lodging of my soul ;
   How canst Thou deign to enter there ?
   Lord, speak and make me whole.

" I am not worthy : yet, my God,
   How can I say Thee nay ?
   Thee, who did'st give Thy Flesh and Blood,
   My ransom-price to pay.

" O come ! in this sweet morning hour,
   Feed me with Food Divine ;
   And fill with all Thy love and power
   This worthless heart of mine."

𝔏𝔢𝔞𝔟𝔦𝔫𝔤 𝔍𝔢𝔰𝔲𝔰.

S. JOHN XIII. 30.

" He went immediately out, and it was night."

IT was Judas who went out into the night, away from Jesus; loving darkness better than light, because his deeds were evil. Look at the contrast offered by that scene. There is S. John lying on the breast of Jesus, in the light of God's own presence, the True Light that lighteth every man that cometh into the world. And there is Judas going away from that presence, away from the Blessed Sacrament of the Lord's Supper, away from peace, and love, and truth ; going out into the darkness of sin and despair, going to betray Jesus. What awful feelings must have been working in the heart of Judas! What reproachful memories must have come crowding upon him! Did not those pleading eyes, that gentle voice, those acts of love and mercy whisper to his heart and say, " Come back ?" It was too late. The devil had entered into Judas. He went out from Jesus, and it was night! Ah! how dark, how black and cold a night for him ! A night of sin and ingratitude, without one star of hope to brighten it ; a night followed by death, by suicide, self-murder. My brothers, those of us who go away from the Presence of the Lord Jesus, from the vows of their baptism, from their prayers, from their Church, from their Bible, go into the night, the black night of sin. Judas went away from Jesus to betray Him. So does the sinner now. The young man or woman who goes away from a life of purity, who sins with his body, betrays the Lord Jesus, and sins against the Body of Jesus. The kiss of impurity is as the kiss of the betrayer on the Face of Jesus. Sins of lust are as the blows and spitting on the Face of Jesus. O young man or woman, if you lead another into sin, you betray the innocent blood, you trample on the Blood of Christ. And these sins end in death, in suicide. Every sinner who goes on sinning, *kills himself*, because God desireth not the death of a sinner. But many of you will say, we have not committed these sins, we have not gone away from Jesus. Stay for a moment, and I will show you that you do go away from His Presence Sunday after Sunday. Week after week Jesus is despised and rejected by those who turn away from the Altar, and leave the Church with the many, whilst the few remain. The Church is filled with people, many of them earnest, godly people, who are trying to lead good lives, and yet they turn away from Jesus present in the Blessed Sacrament, as though they had no part or lot in the matter. These people tell us that they can do very well without Holy Communion. They are Church-goers, they lead decent lives, and therefore they think all is well. But all the while they are acting in direct disobedience to the command of Jesus. He says to us, " do this,"—" take, eat, this is my Body." And many of us will not. And yet these persons profess to love the Lord Jesus. Love, however, is proved by obedience. You would not believe in the affection of your child if he systematically refused to obey you. So our Master says to us, " If ye love Me, keep My commandments." Again, to refuse to come to Holy Communion is not only an act of disobedience, but an act of folly. If you reject that Holy Food you starve your souls. Jesus says in the most plain words, " Unless ye eat the Flesh of the Son of Man, and drink His Blood, you have no life in you.

My brethren, those of us who come to Church, but are not Communicants, are trying to make a bargain with God. They are saying, in fact, I will keep such and such commandments, I will pray, I will read my Bible, I will come to Church, but I will not do what Jesus tells me distinctly to do, I will not " do this." Let us see what it is which keeps people back from the Altar of their Lord. First, there are those people who though Church-goers, do not thoroughly believe or understand the doctrines of the Church. These are the people who are attracted by a popular preacher, or a beautiful service; and having no fixed *principles* of religion, they wander about from the Church to the Meeting-house, and say it is all the same. They naturally do not attach much importance to the Blessed Sacrament. They tell us that it is only a memorial of the death of Christ, and so they would be no better for receiving it. Or they tell us that they might just as well sit round a table at home and break bread, as the Apostles did. We have no need of an altar, they say, nor of any of the mystery and reverence which surrounds the Sacrament. Well, all this would be true enough if this Sacrament were nothing *more* than a memorial, for then it would be an act of piety, but not a Sacrament. But this Sacrament *is* something more. Those who quote the words of our Saviour, " Do this in *remembrance of Me*," ignore those other words of His, "Take, eat, this is My Body; drink ye all of this, for this is My Blood of the New Testament." If the Blessed Sacrament were nothing more than a memorial rite, and if the elements in that Sacrament were nothing more than bread and wine, I could understand why people should regard it lightly; but when we believe, as the Church always has believed, that Jesus Christ is really and truly present in that Holy Sacrament ; that He comes to us then really, though spiritually, and feeds our souls, and pardons our sins, so " that our sinful bodies may be made clean by His body, and our souls washed through

His most precious Blood," then it seems to me madness, suicide, to stay away from the life of our souls. And again, we must remember that the Blessed Sacrament is a sacrifice, and hence it is that "we have an altar," and that the Christian Church has its Priests, as the Jewish Church had. The Jew was looking forward to the coming of the Saviour, and as often as he offered a lamb in sacrifice it was as a type or shadow of the Lamb of God, which was to be sacrificed for the sins of the people. The Christian Priest looks back to that Sacrifice on the Cross, and as often as he celebrates Holy Communion it is as a memorial of that One Sacrifice. The Jew of old did not think as often as he offered a lamb that Christ was offered, neither does the Christian imagine that he repeats " the full, perfect, and sufficient sacrifice, oblation and satisfaction, for the sins of the whole world," when he commemorates these in the Christian Sacrifice. But as the Jewish Priest in his sacrifice pleaded the One Sacrifice which was to come, so do we plead that One Sacrifice which has been offered at Calvary. But there are others to whom I would speak, who believe in the sanctity and power of the Sacrament on the Altar, yet stay away from it. They are not fit to come, they tell us. If by " fitness " they mean *worthiness*, then I answer the best of men is not worthy to draw near to the Sinless Jesus. It is the feeling of our weakness, our liability to do wrong, our unworthiness, which makes the only real fitness for coming to Holy Communion. When we kneel at the Altar we do not say, " We are worthy, O Lord, to kneel at Thy Table, we are very good, earnest people ;" no, we say, " We are not worthy so much as to gather up the crumbs under Thy Table ; we do not presume to come trusting in our own righteousness, but in Thy manifold and great mercies." There is not a word in the whole service about our having reached a certain stage of holiness, a certain degree of goodness which entitles us to come; rather we declare that we come knowing our sinfulness, acknowledging our wretchedness, seeking pardon for the past, and strength to do better in the future.

> " I am not worthy, Holy Lord,
> That Thou should'st come to me ;
> Speak but the Word ; one gracious Word
> Can set the sinner free.

> " I am not worthy ; cold and bare,
> The lodging of my soul;
> How can'st Thou deign to enter there ?
> Lord, speak and make me whole.

> " I am not worthy : yet, my God,
> How can I say Thee nay ?
> Thee, who did'st give Thy Flesh and Blood,
> My ransom-price to pay."

But perhaps you answer me that you do not mean that sort of fitness. Holy Communion is so solemn and

sacred a thing, you say, that if you became a Communicant you would have to lead a very different sort of life,
and to alter many things in your conduct. Now I
understand you. If it would be necessary to alter your
way of life, why do you *not* alter it ? If there is something wrong in your way of living, why do you not change
it ? If you are " not fit " for Holy Communion, whose
fault is it ? Surely your own. Do you think, my
brethren, that you are free to lead this kind of life, which
you say is not quite right, because you are not a Communicant ? Do you imagine that those who come to the
Blessed Sacrament must lead one kind of life, and that
those who come to Church, but not to the Altar, are free
to lead another kind of life ? Believe me, there is only
one kind of life for all God's people. If you are not fit
to be a Communicant, you are not fit to come to Church,
and to be called a Christian. You will say to me, " that
is so different." But you are wrong. You come to
Church to praise and worship God, to confess your sins,
to obtain absolution, to ask for help, to gain strength
and comfort for your soul. All these things are done and
given in the highest sense in the service of Holy Communion. If you are unfit for one, you are unfit for the
other. What is required of those who come to Holy
Communion ? They must *examine* themselves, not to
see if they are free from sin, but to find out whether they
repent truly of their sins. This self-examination, con-

fession of sins, and repentance, are equally required from all Church-goers.   Next, those who come to Holy Communion must *steadfastly purpose to lead a new life;* they must desire to do better to-morrow than they have done to-day.   This applies equally to all of you who come to Church.   If you are quite satisfied with your present life, you could not have meant what you said just now, "We have erred and strayed from Thy ways like lost sheep, we have offended against Thy holy laws."   Next, it is required of Communicants that they should have *a lively faith in God's mercy through Christ.*   This again applies to you all.   If you have not this faith in God's mercy, why are you here in Church?   Next, we are required to *have a thankful remembrance of Christ's death.*   This also is required of all Church-goers; for if the Cross of Jesus is not the beginning and the end of all our hopes for pardon, what meaning can this Service have for us? And once more, we are *to be in charity with all men.* This certainly applies to all Christian people.   Do you think that you are free to come to Church, and to praise God, and pray to Him, and yet harbour unkindly feelings against your neighbour?   Do you think you can ask God "to forgive you your trespasses *as* you forgive those who trespass against you," without blasphemy, if you do not forgive others?   Do you suppose that if you stay away from Holy Communion you are free to hate your brother?   No, believe me, there is the same *fitness* required for Church-going as for being a Communicant; the one ought to mean the other. If there is anything in your lives which keeps you away from the Altar, and which you are unwilling to give up, then remember that sin keeps you away from God, away from salvation, and you will not escape the punishment of your sins, because you turn away from the Blessed Sacrament. Again, I say, there is only one kind of life for all God's people; an earnest striving after holiness. God nowhere tells us that some people are to lead better lives than others; He says to *all*, " Be ye holy." We are all One Family, we have all One Pattern, the Example of the Lord Jesus Christ; One Baptism, One Food, one end and hope to look to. Let no one say, " these words are not for me;" they *are* for you. Let no one say, " this Sacrament is not for me;" it *is* for you, since Jesus died for you. Do not make idle excuses. Do not say that the Holy Sacrament is so mysterious that you cannot understand it. There is no need for you to understand it; your spiritual lives are full of mystery, the world around you is full of mystery; "God is a God who hides Himself." Only believe that Jesus can and will strengthen you in that Blessed Sacrament. That He will be present there on the Altar; that He will give to the poorest and weakest of you just the strength which you need to overcome temptation. I have read of a poor, hard-working woman, who was a regular Communicant, and who had

to suffer much insult and ridicule from godless neighbours.
One day they asked her if she understood the mystery of
the Sacrament, or if she really knew that it did her good.
And she answered humbly that she did not understand
so great a mystery : but she added, " I know what good
I get from it, I go up empty, and I come down full."
There are two classes of people to whom I have been
speaking. The one class is indifferent about the matter,
ready to go on in the old way, and to take their chance ;
not willing to give up something which they know to be
wrong. To these people I say, if you are not fit for
Holy Communion through your own fault, neither are you
fit to be called God's people, nor to die and await the
Judgment. The other class is made up of people who
believe, who are half inclined to come to the Altar, but
who are nervous and uncertain about it. To them I
say, pray that God may show you *now* your need of the
Saviour in the Blessed Sacrament. Then make a resolu-
tion—" I will arise, and go to Jesus when next He calls
me lovingly to His Altar."

If there are any here who were once Communicants,
but have fallen away ; if, like Judas, they have gone from
the light of Christ's presence into the night ; to them, I
say, come back to the light, come back penitent, and
find rest once more with Jesus. If you are weak and
would be strong, if you are sorely tried and tempted, and
would be more patient, more gentle, more self-denying :

if you are sad and need comfort, come to Jesus in the Sacrament of His Love, and say—

" Just as I am,
Without one plea,
But that Thy Blood was shed for me,
And that Thou bid'st me come to Thee,
O Lamb of God, I come."

K

" The Church's One foundation
Is Jesus Christ her Lord;
She is His new creation,
By water and the word :
From Heaven He came and sought her
To be His holy Bride ;
With His own Blood He bought her,
And for her life He died.

" Elect from every nation,
Yet one o'er all the earth,
Her charter of salvation
One Lord, one faith, one birth ;
One Holy Name she blesses,
Partakes one Holy Food,
And to one hope she presses
With every grace endued.

" Though with a scornful wonder
Men see her sore opprest,
By schisms rent asunder,
By heresies distrest,
Yet saints their watch are keeping,
Their cry goes up, ' How long ?'
And soon the night of weeping
Shall be the morn of song.

" 'Mid toil and tribulation,
And tumult of her war,
She waits the consummation
Of peace for evermore ;
Till with the vision glorious
Her longing eyes are blest,
And the great Church victorious
Shall be the Church at rest.

" Yet she on earth hath union
With God the Three in One,
And mystic, sweet communion
With those whose rest is won :
O happy ones and holy !
Lord, give us grace that we,
Like them the meek and lowly,
On high may dwell with Thee.

SERMON XVI.

The One Foundation.

COLOSSIANS I. 18.

" He is the head of the body, the Church."

WHEN the world was drowned by the flood, God saved a faithful remnant, His Church, and kept it safe in the Ark. To that Church He gave His Covenant, and sent it forth into the world to propagate the true faith from generation to generation. From the very first the leading principle of the Church was unity, *oneness.* It was to be one, holy, universal Church, composed of *one* people, all having *one* language, *one* Covenant. And God's will is the same now. His Church has one faith, one Baptism, one language, that is, one doctrine, all over the world. In those early days, when Noah's descendants formed the Church of God, man's pride and ignorance caused a division, or schism, in the Church. The unity of the Body was broken by the pride and folly of the dwellers in the plains of Shinar, who said, " Go to, let us build us a city and a tower, whose top shall reach unto Heaven, and let us make us a name."

The tower which they built was probably intended for some idolatrous purpose. God had saved the people, and had bidden them to worship in a particular manner. But their pride stood in the way. They wished to make themselves a name, other than the name of God's Church. They preferred to worship God in their own way, instead of in God's way. They determined to be guided by their own ideas, instead of by God's commands, and to found a religious society of their own, in place of that which was Divine.

Thus we get the first instance of schism, the first break in the unity of the Church. And what was the result? Just what always follows schism, confusion and strife. God looked on the work of those Babel builders, and confounded their language, so that they could not understand one another. They had built this tower that they might not be scattered over the earth, and their act brought about the very result which they dreaded. Now there is a very plain lesson for us to be learnt from this history of an old dead and gone sin. Our country to-day is like the plain of Shinar, where men are busy building Babels. One thinks that he will make himself a name, another that he will reach Heaven by a way of his own. And the end of all these Babels is confusion and destruction. They are built as monuments of pride, and presently the tower which they made so strong for themselves falls, and great is the fall thereof. There are those who build a Worldly Babel. "Let us make a name," they say. So they live lavishly, spend money beyond their means, encourage their children in extravagance, till suddenly the tower falls, and they are overwhelmed in the ruins of bankruptcy. Another Babel-builder is the man who makes his business the one great object of his life, who determines that he will make money at any cost; honestly if he can, if not, still it shall be made. He tells us that he does not object to religion, but it must not stand in the way of his work. It must not come between him and a hard bargain, or even an unjust act. His way is the way of the world. The laws of God, the rules of the Church, are not for practical men like him, but for Priests and women. Ah! foolish builder, your work is only a Tower of Babel. You are hoping to make yourself a name, and are heaping up riches without knowing who shall gather them. What if the son for whom you have laboured becomes a spendthrift and a prodigal? How will your work profit you then? When you die, what will your money profit you then? The Babel falls to ruins.

"Go to, let us make us a name." So speak the Babel-builders of to-day. One desires the name of a sharp man of business, another the name of a millionaire. One covets the name of a clever sceptic; he has discovered that the Bible is all a mistake, and that a belief in God, or in Prayer, is old-fashioned and out of date. He would have us believe in *him* rather than in God. And for these men the day comes when they lie among the ruins of their Babel. They hoped to make them a name, and they have failed to gain the only name which endures, one which is written in Heaven.

Again, there are those who build religious Babels. They say, " Go to, let us build us a city and a tower, whose top may reach unto Heaven." They would reach Heaven by a way of their own making. The history of schism, from the time of the Tower of Babel to this day, has always been the same. Men build Towers of Babel, and the result is confusion, division, strife. Brethren, we as members of Christ's Church are members of *One* Body, and to cause division or separation in that Body is grievous sin. If we wander away from the Church, and seek some form of religion of our own choosing; if we break the unity of the Church, the Family in which we " are all one in Christ Jesus ;" if, having itching ears, we follow first one teacher, then another, in various sects, all more or less opposed to each other, and all opposed to the Church, we commit a great sin. We create confusion, where God would have order; we rend the seamless robe of Christ, which even the soldiers spared. Those who separate themselves from the Church, and join some religious society of man's making, are merely building a Tower of Babel, and saying, " let us make us a tower which will reach unto Heaven." And the end of this is confusion and division.

In the Church all are of one speech. The same holy faith is proclaimed, the same holy Sacraments administered wherever the Catholic Church is found. But among the various Sects which have parted from the Church there is confusion of tongues, so that a man cannot understand his neighbour. One Sect holds one doctrine about holy Baptism for instance, another maintains exactly the opposite view, and yet each of these religious bodies declares that it is teaching the truth as it is in Christ Jesus, and preaching the Gospel. I am not now speaking to those who have never been taught Church principles. I speak to you who profess to be members of Christ's Holy Church, and I want you to realize the sin of dividing yourselves, and separating from the One Family, the Communion of Saints, the Church in Paradise and in earth, whilst you strive to build a Babel of your own. "Other foundation can no man lay than is laid, which is Jesus Christ;"—"He is the head of the Body, the Church."

> " The Church's one foundation
> Is Jesus Christ her Lord,
> She is His new creation,
> By water and the word :
> From Heaven He came and sought her
> To be His holy Bride;
> With His own Blood He bought her,
> And for her life He died."

We have seen the Church, founded on the Apostles and Prophets, Jesus Christ being the head corner-stone, remaining unchanged, in spite of persecution and unbelief. We have seen, too, endless heresies, and unnumbered sects arise, and then pass away. Let us learn then that Babel falls, but the City of our God stands firm. What man does will fail, what God does shall endure for ever.

" King of Saints, to whom the number
    Of Thy starry host is known,
    Many a name, by man forgotten,
    Lives for ever round Thy throne ;
    Lights, which earth-born mists have darkened,
    There are shining full and clear,
    Princes in the courts of Heaven,
    Nameless, unremembered here.

" In the roll of Thine Apostles,
    One there stands, Bartholomew,
    He to whom to-day we offer,
    Year by year, our praises due ;
    How he toiled for Thee and suffered
    None on earth can now record ;
    All his saintly life is hidden
    In the knowledge of his Lord.

" Was it he, beneath the fig-tree
    Seen of Thee, and guileless found ;
    He who saw the good he longed for,
    Rise from Nazareth's barren ground ;
    He who met his risen Master
    On the shore of Galilee ;
    He to whom the word was spoken,
    ' Greater things thou yet shalt see ?'

" None can tell us ; all is written
    In the Lamb's great book of life,
    All the faith, and prayer, and patience,
    All the toiling, and the strife ;
    There are told Thy hidden treasures ;
    Number us, O Lord, with them,
    When Thou makest up the jewels
    Of Thy living diadem."

SERMON XVII.

Unknown, yet Well Known.

(FESTIVAL OF S. BARTHOLOMEW.)

2 TIMOTHY II. 19.

" The Lord knoweth them that are His."

MANY of the greatest Saints have lived and died unknown and uncared for by the world. These are God's secret ones, unknown to men, well-known to God. About some of the Saints and Apostles we hear much; the lives and works of S. Paul and S. Peter are familiar to us all. It is not so with S. Bartholomew, and yet none of the Martyrs worked more faithfully, or suffered more severely. What we do know of him is gathered chiefly from sources outside the Bible. He is supposed to have been the same as Nathaniel, a native of Galilee, and at the time of his call, a young fisherman. Bartholomew is closely connected with S. Philip, who first brought him to Jesus; and with his teacher he worked and preached till S. Philip became a martyr. When he was told that Jesus of Nazareth was the Messiah, Bartholomew doubted, wondering how any good thing could come out of a town in hated and despised Galilee, but when once he came to Jesus he remained faithful even unto death. After our Lord's Ascension, and after the descent of the Holy Ghost at Pentecost, Bartholomew is said to have begun his Mission by preaching in Northern India. Among the wild and fierce people of that distant land he made many converts. In the Second Century of the Christian era a Missionary in India was shown a Hebrew copy of S. Matthew's Gospel, said to have been given to the ancestors of the Christians there by S. Bartholomew. Travelling to the west and north of Asia, S. Bartholomew, in company with S. Philip, came to Hierapolis, a city of Phrygia, and showed the people there the folly of their idol worship; many persons being converted to the faith. This excited the anger of the authorities, and two crosses were prepared for the preachers of the Cross of Christ. S. Philip was actually put to death; S. Bartholomew was bound to the cross, and prepared to yield up his guileless soul to God, when fear, or repentance moved the people, and they let him go free. Thus S. Bartholomew was, on this occasion, a martyr in will, but not in deed. The time came when he was a martyr both in will and deed. Once more he went forth to his work and to his labour until the evening of death. Having preached successfully in Lycaonia, he went to Armenia, and there the king of that region was converted, his wife and subjects following

his example. Bartholomew bought these souls for Christ
at the price of his own blood. The idolatrous priests
persuaded the brother of the converted king to put the
Apostle to death, and he suffered martyrdom for the
second time at a city on the shores of the Caspian Sea.
It is said that he was flayed alive, according to the bar-
barous custom of the country, and afterwards crucified.
Yet he who laboured so successfully for Christ, and
suffered so severely, is only mentioned four times in the
New Testament, and then very slightly. There is no
word to record his hard toil, his burning love, his patient
suffering, and his noble death.

> " How he toiled for Thee and suffered,
>   None on earth can now record ;
>   All his saintly life is hidden
>   In the knowledge of his Lord."

And so it is with many of the greatest of God's saints.
No one knows the name of Naaman's little servant, who
brought her Master to God. The names of the Holy
Innocents appear in no earthly book. That pious widow
who gave all she had to the Temple is not named ; and
there are thousands of others, who though " unknown,
are well known " to God, whose names are not written on
earth, but are written in Heaven. There are many who
are now living for God, and working for Him, and
suffering for Him, of whom this world knows nothing.

There are Clergy labouring in obscure parishes, who have
never been heard of in the great world of London, who
will never be rich, who will be promoted, but who will
work faithfully for their Master, Jesus, till the evening,
and then go to rest under the shadow of the old Church.
Their names are unknown to fame, but they are written
in Heaven,—"the Lord knoweth them that are His."
There are Missionaries serving their Master in foreign
lands among the heathen, amid dangers, hardships and
death. When they die, perhaps a violent death, no
notice will be taken of them. There will not be, perhaps,
a paragraph about them in the newspapers, but "the
Lord knoweth them that are His."

Now think of yourselves. You all have a work to do
for Christ, and a life to live for Him. For most of you
that life will be one of obscurity. Your names will never
be published to the world ; you will live and die quietly
among your native woods and hills, and within the sound
of your own Church bells. But if you are trying to lead
a good life, and are helping others to do so, then though
your names may be unknown to the world, they are well
known to God. Every victory which you have won over
sin and temptation, though unknown to men, is known
to God. Every time you have denied yourself for the
sake of others ; every time you have done a kindly act
for Christ's dear sake, God knew it, these things are
noted in His book. The world knows nothing about the

simple old cottager who, in spite of poverty and rheu-
matism, and failing sight, is yet cheerful and contented,
and blesses God for his daily bread. But God knows all
about that simple saint of His. The world knows
nothing of the hard-worked, much-tried man or woman
who kneels regularly at the Altar of Holy Communion;
but Jesus, present there, sees and welcomes that humble
worshipper. Your way of life may be far from the noise,
and stir, and energy of the great world, your light may
be set to shine in a corner; your struggles, your sorrows,
your prayers may be all unknown to men, but they are
well known to God.

God has hidden saints in every place, dwelling under
cottage thatch, as well as in great houses. These are the
gems which no earthly eye has ever valued, but they will
shine none the less brightly on that day when God makes
up His jewels. Of the story of such lives men know
nothing, but

> " . . . . all is written
> In the Lamb's great book of Life,
> All the faith, and prayer, and patience,
> All the toiling, and the strife ;
> There are told Thy hidden treasures ;
> Number us, O Lord, with them,
> When Thou makest up the jewels
> Of Thy living diadem."

" Dear Lord, on this Thy servant's day,
　Who left for Thee the gold and mart,
　Who heard Thee whisper, ' Come away,'
　And followed with a single heart.

" Give us, amid earth's weary moil,
　And wealth for which men cark and care,
　'Mid fortune's pride, and need's wild toil,
　And broken hearts in purple rare,

" Give us Thy grace to rise above
　The glare of this world's smelting fires ;
　Let God's great love put out the love
　Of gold, and gain, and low desires.

" Still, like a breath from scented lime,
　Borne into rooms where sick men faint,
　His voice comes floating through all time,
　Thine own Evangelist and Saint.

" Still sweetly rings the Gospel strain
　Of golden store that knows not rust,
　The love of Christ is more than gain,
　And heavenly crowns than yellow dust.

SERMON XVIII.

Treasure in Heaven.

(Festival of S. Matthew.)

S. Matthew VI. 20.

" Lay up for yourselves treasures in heaven."

WHAT do we know of S. Matthew, whose festival we celebrate to-day, and what lessons can we learn from his life ? Matthew, or Levi, was the son of Alphæus, and probably a native of Galilee. He was a publican or tax-gatherer, and his special duty was to collect the dues and customs paid on the cargoes of vessels which crossed the sea of Tiberias. The publicans were a class hateful to the Jews, first, because they were the servants of the Romans, and next, because they farmed the taxes from the Roman government at a fixed price, and tried to enrich themselves by injustice and extortion. There were two classes of publicans, a superior order of which Zaccheus is the type, and an inferior class of collectors, of whom Matthew was one. Doubtless S. Matthew was well off, like most of his order ; for both the upper and

L

lower class of Publicans made as much profit as possible
from the taxes. The summons of Jesus, " Follow Me,"
meant therefore to S. Matthew a great sacrifice of self.
It meant giving up what he already had, and the chance
of acquiring much more. For plenty he would have
poverty, in place of rich and powerful masters he would
have a Master who had nowhere to lay His Head, who
was despised and rejected of men, All this was meant
by following Jesus. And S. Matthew made his choice, and
became one of those blessed ones, who are " poor, yet
making many rich, having nothing, and yet possessing
all things." He learned to feel—

> " What is the gold of all this world but dross,
>   The joy but sorrow, and the pleasure pain ;
>   The wealth but beggary, and the gain but loss,
>   The wit but folly, and the virtue vain;
>   Thus, since to Heaven compared, the world is such
>   What thing is man to love the world so much ?"

S. Matthew gave up the gold of this world, but he had
found treasure in Heaven, even the goodly pearl of great
price ; and to gain this he willingly sacrificed all else.
For eight years after our Lord's Ascension, S. Matthew
preached to his brethren in Judæa ; and before setting
forth to preach the Gospel to the Gentiles, he was urged
to write the story of Christ's life and works. Hence we
get the Gospel of St. Matthew, written expressly for the
Jews, and therefore in Hebrew, although it was soon

translated into Greek by an unknown hand. Having
finished this task, the Evangelist went to Egypt and
Ethiopia. S. Chrysostom says, in reference to his success,
that "he washed the Ethiopian white." He is said to
have suffered martyrdom in Ethiopia, but the manner of his
death is not known.

And now let us learn the lessons which spring from
S. Matthew's life.

" Dear Lord, on this Thy servant's day,
Who left for Thee the gold and mart,
Who heard Thee whisper, ' Come away,'
And followed with a single heart ;

" Give us, amid earth's weary moil,
And wealth for which men cark and care,
'Mid fortune's pride, and need's wild toil,
And broken hearts in purple rare,

" Give us Thy grace to rise above
The glare of this world's smelting fires ;
Let God's great love put out the love
Of gold, and gain, and low desires."

S. Matthew let nothing stand between him and Jesus,
he gave up all, and followed Him. He forms a strong
contrast to the young Ruler, who came to Jesus, but
without counting the cost, and so went away sorrowful.
There are many so-called Christians among us now, who
have not counted the cost of following Jesus, who are not
prepared to give up anything for Christ's sake. Believe

me, brethren, you can't have Jesus Christ and your own
way too. There is the mistake which so many of us
make. We try to make God's Will fit in with our
selfish wishes, instead of making God's Will our will.
But some man will say, " How impractical all this is !
Do you wish me to give up my farm, or my merchandize,
to forsake my business, and become a beggar ?" Certainly
not. God does not require this of you. But He *does*
require you to give up whatever hinders you from being
a Christian ; whatever keeps you back from holiness,
however dear it may be to you. If a man says to me,
"My land occupies so much of my time that I have
scarcely any opportunity for religion ;" then I say, "that
land of yours is lying between you and the Better Land of
Heaven." If you are saying in answer to the call of
Jesus, "I have bought a piece of land, and therefore I
cannot come," you must alter this. You must think of
God first, and your land afterwards; you must put your
soul before your farm, otherwise at the last you will have
six feet of earth for your worn-out body, and you will have
lost your soul. If a tradesman says, " My business wont
let me be honest ;" then I tell him that he must give up
that business, or conduct it in a different way, or he cannot
be Christ's servant. If a man or woman says, "I stay
away from Holy Communion because there is some
pleasure, or habit, which I know to be wrong, but which
I don't like to give up ;" then let such an one know that

he is staying away from Jesus, and suffering this darling sin to stand between him and his Saviour. Brethren, make your choice. Will you give up what you know to be wrong, or will you give up everlasting life ? I knew a man who made his choice, but not as S. Matthew did. He had knelt many a time at the Altar, and received the Blessed Sacrament from these hands of mine; but he fell into sin, and when urged to forsake it, he answered, " I will not, if it costs me my soul." So he made his choice. Your own conscience will tell you in each individual case, what is keeping you back from being altogether Christ's servant. Look into your hearts now while I speak ; ask yourselves the question, " What must I give up for Christ ? What keeps me back from Him in my daily life, in my pleasures, in my work ?" Find out what obstacle there is between you and Jesus, and then ask Him to give you strength to pluck it out, and to cast it from you. It is better for us to enter into life maimed, and deprived of some darling sin, than having had our own way to the last to be cast out from God's presence for ever.

" Still sweetly rings the Gospel strain,
Of golden store that knows not rust ;
The love of Christ is more than gain,
And heavenly crowns than yellow dust."

" How sweet the Name of Jesus sounds,
    In a believer's ear !
    It soothes his sorrows, heals his wounds,
    And drives away his fear.

" It makes the wounded spirit whole,
    And calms the troubled breast ;
    'Tis manna to the hungry soul,
    And to the weary rest.

" Dear Name! the rock on which I build,
    My shield and hiding-place,
    My never-failing treasury filled
    With boundless stores of grace.

" Jesus ! my Shepherd, Husband, Friend,
    My Prophet, Priest, and King,
    My Lord, my Life, my Way, my End,
    Accept the praise I bring.

" Weak is the effort of my heart,
    And cold my warmest thought ;
    But when I see Thee as Thou art,
    I'll praise Thee as I ought.

" Till then I would Thy love proclaim
    With every fleeting breath ;
    And may the music of Thy Name
    Refresh my soul in death."

SERMON XIX.

The Shadows and the Substance.

(For a Children's Service.)

S. John v. 39.

" Search the Scriptures ; for in them ye think ye have eternal life : and they are they which testify of Me."

I am going to talk to you, my children, about reading the Bible. I hope many of you read the Bible because you love it. Some of you, perhaps, read it as a task, and without interest. Now, if I were to ask you why we ought to study God's Book, you would tell me rightly that we do so to learn about God's holy will and commandments. But what does our Lord Jesus Christ say about Bible reading? He tells us to search the Scriptures, because they testify, or bear witness, of Him. When our Lord said this did He refer to the New Testament? Certainly not, because it had not yet been written. So He tells us that the Old Testament bears witness of Him. Perhaps many of you children, like a good many older people, have only looked for Jesus in the New Testament. You may have thought that the Old Testament is a hard book, very unlike the "sweet story of old," which we hear in the Gospel. You may have looked upon it only as the history of the Jews, and their laws, and their battles, and their kings and judges. But if you read the Old Testament properly you will see Jesus Christ there. Have you ever seen a photographic artist take one of those sun-pictures which are now so common? Well, at first there was no picture to be seen, only a piece of glass with a kind of white cloud upon it. But presently as the artist poured certain chemicals upon it, a picture began to come out of the mist; first one feature, then another, till you saw the likeness of a friend. The Old Testament scriptures sometimes appear strange and uninteresting to you, there is a mist over them as it were. But as you study the words, or hear them explained, gradually new beauties, new features come out, and you find a likeness. Whose likeness, my children? The likeness of Jesus Christ, the Friend of little children. I dare say none of you ever saw a kind of ink used for secret writing. Common ink, you know, leaves a very plain mark on the paper; but this ink, of which I am speaking, fades away directly after it is used, and the paper seems to be blank. But if that sheet of paper is held to the fire, the writing comes out, and can be read easily. Now to a great many people the pages of the Bible, especially of the Old Testament, seem all blank,

without any beauty or interest.   But if you learn to read
God's word with care and intelligence, above all, if you
pray to God to show you the true meaning, the pages
which seemed blank before will be full of interest for you.
But perhaps you think among yourselves, how can we
find Jesus in the Old Testament, when we do not read
of His Birth till we come to the Gospels?   I will try to
show you what I mean.   If you were watching the wall
of the school-lane on a sunny day, when the children
were leaving school, what would you see?   The shadows
of the children.   Yes, and at a certain time of the day
their shadows would be cast before them, so that first
you see the shadow, then the child itself.   Well, when
you read the Old Testament you see the shadow of Jesus,
in the New Testament you see the Substance, Jesus
Himself.   And these shadows of Jesus are called Types.
Thus when we read the books of the Old Testament we
look forward to Jesus coming to die for our sins, and to
rise again for our justification.   When we read the New
Testament we look back at the time when Jesus did
come, and live on this earth, and die on the Cross; and
we look forward also to the time when He shall come
again to judge the quick and the dead.   Now let us open
our Bibles, and look at some of the shadows of Jesus
Christ passing across the pages of the Old Testament.
Look at the story of Abel.   Can you see any shadow of
Jesus Christ there?   What sort of sacrifice did he offer to

God ?   One which was acceptable.   And so Jesus
offered Himself as a Sacrifice for the sins of the whole
world, and it was accepted.   And Abel was slain by his
brother's hand ; and here again we get a type of Jesus
who was put to death by His brethren.   Now think of
Isaac.   He was the child of Promise, the beloved son of
his father.   He was chosen for a sacrifice, and he bore
the wood for that sacrifice to Mount Moriah.   Here is
the shadow ; now at the substance ; see Jesus, the Child
of Promise, the Beloved Son of His Heavenly Father,
carrying the wood of the Cross for His own sacrifice.
Or let us turn to that story which every child loves to
read, the story of Joseph.   Ah ! how plainly you can see
the shadow of Jesus falling there.   Joseph, the beloved
son, is sent to his brethren, and is hated of them.   He
is cast into a pit, and is sold to the Ishmaelites.   He is
put in prison on a false charge, his feet are made fast in
the stocks, the iron enters into his soul.   He is bound
between two malefactors, to the one he promises life, to
the other death.   He is raised up on high, the king sent
and delivered him.   Then he feeds a starving people
with bread, because he was sent before his brethren to
preserve life.   Now in all this, my children, we can see
the story of Jesus Christ.   He, the Beloved Son, is sent
to His brethren in this world to preserve life, to give them
eternal life.   He is hated of His brethren, despised and
rejected of men, He is numbered among the transgressors.

He is sold to His enemies, He is put in prison on a false
charge, He is bound on the Cross between two malefactors, and promises life to one, and leaves the other to
his doom. He is delivered from the prison of the grave,
and is exalted to the right hand of His Father in Heaven ;
and He ever feeds His people with the Bread of Life in
the Blessed Sacrament. Now let us think of Aaron.
Again we see the shadow of Jesus Christ. Aaron was
the High Priest, and Jesus is called " Our great High
Priest, and a Priest for ever after the order of Melchizedek."
What was the special duty of a Priest ? To offer sacrifice.
Can you tell me about a particular day when the High
Priest alone offered a special sacrifice? That day was
the Day of Atonement, and then, on that day only, the
High Priest entered into the Holy of Holies, and offered
a sacrifice for the sins of the people ; sprinkling the blood
of the victim before the mercy-seat. Now, my children,
let us see how this was a shadow of Jesus Christ. He is our
High Priest, He offered a sacrifice for the sins of the
whole world. So our day of Atonement was when that
sacrifice was offered on the Cross, when Jesus was Himself the victim. And can we see no shadow of Jesus as
we look at the High Priest sprinkling the blood before
the mercy-seat, in the Holy of Holies? Jesus has passed
into the Holy of Holies, that is Heaven. What does He
do there for us ? He pleads for us, for the sake of His
Precious Blood poured out for us, He pleads that we

may be forgiven; thus He sprinkles His Blood, as it
were, before the Mercy Seat. Never suppose that our
dear Lord's work was done when He died on the Cross.
He not only *died* for us, but He ever *lives* to make
intercession for us. Let us go on, my children, to think
of some types or shadows of Jesus which are less familiar
to you than these, about which we have spoken so often.
We will look into the Book of Joshua, and there we shall
see in almost every line a shadow of Jesus.

First of all, there is the very name of Joshua, which is
exactly the same name as Jesus, and means, as you all
know, a *Saviour*. When we see Joshua leading God's
people against their enemies, and after conquering them,
dividing the land of Canaan among the children of Israel,
do we not see the shadow of *our* Joshua, the Lord Jesus
Christ? What are the enemies which He conquered for
us? Sin and death. What enemies does He help us to
conquer now? The world, the flesh, and the devil; all
the temptations and bad thoughts which come to us.
And does not our Joshua promise us a good land, which
He will divide among His people? Yes, surely, the good
land of Heaven, whither He says He is gone to prepare
a place for us. We read in the beginning of this book
how Joshua was appointed to succeed Moses, who had
given the people the law. So we turn from the shadow
and see the Substance; we see Jesus Christ sent to do
what the law could not do, to save the people. I dare

say some of you can tell me a text about this? " The law was given by Moses, but grace and truth came by Jesus Christ." Moses, with all his wisdom and goodness, could not save the people from their enemies in Canaan, nor was he even allowed to pass over Jordan into the Promised Land. Joshua was chosen to do this. So we know that " there is no other name given among men whereby we must be saved," but the name of our Joshua, Jesus Christ. So we do right to sing—

> " How sweet the name of Jesus sounds
> In a believer's ear !
> It soothes his sorrows, heals his wounds,
> And drives away his fear.

> " Dear Name ! the rock on which I build,
> My shield and hiding-piace,
> My never-failing treasury filled
> With boundless stores of grace."

Do you remember, children, how the children of Israel passed over Jordan? The Priests bore the Ark of God, and as soon as their feet were dipped in the waters of Jordan, the waters flowed backward, and the people passed over. There we get the shadow of Jesus Christ, our·great High Priest, who dipped His feet in the river of death, which lies between us and the Better Land, and then a way was made for us to pass over, since Jesus says, " Whosoever liveth and believeth in Me shall never die." And do you remember how Joshua chose twelve men from the twelve tribes to carry twelve stones over with them? Well, here we get a shadow of Jesus choosing the twelve Apostles, who were to be the foundation stones of His Church. It was on the same day of the month as that on which Jesus rode in triumph into Jerusalem, that Joshua began his march to victory. That day of our Lord's entry into Jerusalem is called Palm Sunday, because the people strewed palm branches, the sign of victory, in the way. Now can you tell me what was Joshua's first victory? It was at Jericho, the city of Palm trees. Thus far you see, my children, how the features of the Lord Jesus Christ come out in the pages of the Old Testament. We will look again at these shadows on another occasion.

SERMON XX.

The Shadows and the Substance.

(FOR A CHILDREN'S SERVICE.)

S. JOHN V. 39.

*" Search the scriptures, for in them ye think ye have eternal life ;
and they are they which testify of Me."*

THERE was once a famous artist who made a wonderful
shield, and worked his own name so cleverly into it,
that it could not be removed without destroying the
shield. The Bible is like that shield, and the name of
Jesus is so worked into it, that we find it everywhere.
Let us think now of the life of David, who is a most
perfect type of Jesus. First of all, my children, think
where David was born. In Bethlehem, the same place
where Jesus was born in the aftertime. David was of
the tribe of Judah, and of a noble race, for Jesse, his
father, was descended from one who had been a Prince
in the time of Moses. But when David was born, his
family was poor, and he seemed the least of those whom
he called his brethren. So our Blessed Lord, born of

the tribe of Judah, possessing all the riches of Heaven, "became poor, that He might make many rich;" and we know that He was despised, and seemed as the least among those whom He called His brethren. Next, we know that David was a shepherd, and is not that one of our Lord's names? Yes, the Good Shepherd who layeth down His life for the sheep. "We are the people of His pasture, and the sheep of His Hand." Can you tell me, children, how many times David was anointed? Three times; first at Bethlehem, secondly at Hebron, as king over Judah, and again, after seven years, as king over all Israel. Now the persons who were anointed were, as you know, Prophets, Priests, and Kings, and our Saviour was all three, and so may be said to have been thrice anointed, as a Priest for ever, that Prophet which should come into the world, and as the King of Glory. When Jesse, the father of David, sent him to the camp to see how his brethren fared, and to take them food, he was badly received by them. When God the Father sent His Son into the world, not only to see how His brethren fared, but to deliver them, and to give them the True Food, the Bread of Life, He too was badly received. They said of Jesus, "Away with Him, away with Him;" the brethren of His own household called Him mad. David answered his brethren gently, saying, "What have I now done, is there not a cause?" So Jesus, "when He was reviled, reviled not again," and "as a lamb before her shearers, so He opened not His mouth." You all know the story of the giant Goliath, and how David the shepherd boy slew him. Well, we see there the shadow of Jesus Christ. Goliath, the Philistine giant, the enemy of Israel, is a type of Satan, the giant of wickedness, the enemy of God's people. For forty days Goliath drew near morning and evening, and presented himself. So for forty days Satan presented himself to Jesus in the wilderness of temptation. David refused Saul's armour; and so Jesus took no armour, save that of holiness, for His battle with Satan ; and He won that battle clothed only with our poor, weak flesh. David chose weapons despised of men, a staff, and five smooth stones from the brook. What weapons did our Saviour choose? Can you tell me what His staff was? The Cross. And the five smooth stones were taken from the brook of sorrow, of which He drank in the way, and they were His Five Precious Wounds. David cut off the giant's head with his own sword; and Jesus by His death conquered him who had the power of death; thus did Jesus " bruise the serpent's head " with his own weapon.

Saul had promised great reward to him who should conquer the giant. The promise was that " the king will enrich him with great riches, and will give him his daughter, and make his father's house free in Israel."

And now think of the rewards of our Lord Jesus, the Conqueror of sin and death. He was to be enriched

M

with great riches ; "therefore will I divide Him a portion
with the great." But the reward given to Jesus was not
that of gold and silver. Can you tell me, my children,
what is the most precious thing in His eyes? A soul
that is saved. Yes, Christ's reward was the souls of
His ransomed people. And what, think you, was the
Bride, the king's daughter, " all glorious within," which
was to be given to Jesus? Do we not read of the Bride
many times in the Bible? In the Book of Revelation,
for instance, we read, " The Spirit and the Bride say,
come !" Who is meant by the Bride of Christ? The
Church ; and it was this Holy Bride which Jesus gained
by His victory over Satan. And it was promised too,
that His Father's house should be made free in Israel.
This too was fulfilled also, for His Heavenly Father's
House was made free from the bondage of sin and
death. You all remember how an evil spirit entered
into Saul, and how David soothed him and healed him
with his music. Now let us look for the shadow of
Jesus here. He came into a sinful world, and found
people troubled by evil spirits, and He healed them.
What was the music of Jesus? The music of the
Gospel, the sweet message, "Come unto me, all ye that
travail and are heavy laden." This was the music which
soothed and comforted the troubled hearts ; and more
than this, we know that He cast out the devils with His
word. When we read about Saul persecuting David,

and how David forgave him, we see a shadow of Jesus persecuted for righteousness sake, and praying for those who did Him wrong. Twice Saul threw a javelin at David, twice the Jews tried to stone Jesus. When we read of Doeg, the Edomite, standing at the holy place before the Lord, and afterwards betraying David, we look from the shadow to the substance, and we see Judas Iscariot, standing before the Lord at the Feast of the Passover, and afterwards betraying Jesus. Or when we see David in the cave of Adullam, and find all the people who had committed crimes, and were in danger, coming to him; we see Jesus in this world, a place like the cave of Adullam, and becoming the "friend of publicans and sinners." Again, later in David's life, we hear of the rebellion of his son Absalom, and there we see a shadow of the Jews rebelling against Jesus, and saying, "We will not have this man to reign over us." David, you will remember, when full of sorrow and trouble at his son's rebellion, departed from Jerusalem, crossed the brook Kidron, ascended the mount of Olives, and wept there; he felt love and compassion for Absalom in spite of his wickedness, and said, "Deal gently, for my sake, with the young man;" he forgave Shimei who cursed him, and would not suffer him to be put to death. Now, my children, look from the shadows to the substance, and you will see Jesus going along the same path in His sorrow, which David had traversed long before. He

crossed the brook Kidron, He wept over Jerusalem from
the mount of Olives, He was betrayed by Judas, as was
David by Ahitophel, He suffered agony of soul in the
Garden, He forgave those who cursed Him, and prayed
for those who had rebelled against Him—" Father, forgive them, for they know not what they do." We will
look at one more shadow now. When the plague was
sent upon Israel, the angel of the Lord was bidden to
stay his hand at the threshing-floor of Araunah, the
Jebusite. Now that threshing-floor was on mount
Moriah. Can you tell me, children, where that was?
At Jerusalem? Yes; and what great event happened
there in the old days? There Abraham took Isaac to
offer him as a sacrifice; and there God chose the spot
for the building of His Temple. David bought the
threshing-floor, and offered peace-offerings there, and the
plague was stayed. Now we look at the substance, and
we see Jesus offering Himself as a sacrifice at Jerusalem,
and staying the plague of sin and death which threatened
the world. Thus the shadows of the Old Testament
lead us all one way, to Bethlehem, and to Calvary; and
as it used to be said of old that "all roads lead to
Rome," so every part of God's Word, if rightly followed,
will lead to Jesus Christ.

" There's a Friend for little children,
Above the bright blue sky,
A Friend who never changes,
Whose love will never die ;
Our earthy friends may fail us,
And change with changing years,
This Friend is always worthy
Of that dear Name He bears.

" There's a rest for little children
Above the bright blue sky,
Who love the Blessèd Saviour,
And to the Father cry ;
A rest from every turmoil,
From sin and sorrow free,
Where every little pilgrim,
Shall rest eternally.

" There's a home for little children
Above the bright blue sky,
And all who look for Jesus
Shall wear it by and by ;
A crown of brightest glory,
Which He will then bestow,
On those who found his favour,
And loved His name below.

" There's a song for little children
Above the bright blue sky,
A song that will not weary,
Though sung continually ;
A song which even angels
Can never, never sing ;
They know not Christ as Saviour,
But worship Him as King.

" There's a robe for little children
Above the bright blue sky,
And a harp of sweetest music,
And palms of victory.
All, all above is treasured,
And found in Christ alone ;
Lord, grant Thy little children,
To know Thee as their own."

SERMON XXI.

The Children's Portion.

(FOR A CHILDREN'S SERVICE.)

S. LUKE IX. 47.

" Jesus took a child, and set him by Him."

THIS hymn, which you all know so well, tells us about the good things which God has prepared for them that love Him. These good things pass man's understanding; and they are prepared for you and all God's children. Let us see then what is the Children's Portion in the good things of Heaven. First, we are told that

> " There's a Friend for little children
> Above the bright blue sky,
> A Friend who never changes,
> Whose love will never die ;
> Our earthly friends may fail us,
> And change with changing years,
> This Friend is always worthy
> Of that dear Name He bears."

Now, how do we know that Jesus is the Children's Friend? We know it because when He was on the earth He commanded the children to be brought to Him, and He rebuked those who would have kept them from Him. He took the children in His arms, and blessed them; on one occasion He took a child, and set him by Him, and told His disciples that none could enter Heaven unless they became like children. Does Jesus ever take little children in His arms now ? Yes, when you were brought to His Holy Baptism, then Jesus took you in His arms, and blessed you, and received you as God's own children by adoption. You, my children, all have friends. He would be a very miserable child indeed who had not at least one friend. You have some one to whom you tell your troubles, and your pleasures ; to whom you show your new toys, to whom you tell any piece of news which interests you. And if that friend is a *true* friend he will be happy if you are happy, and sad if you are in trouble; he will enter into all your feelings, and think more of you than of himself. He will *sympathise* with you. This is what we expect in a real friend. But the greatest thing that a man can do for his friend is to die for him. There have been instances of this devotion between friends. In the French Revolution, when, as some of you know, people were carried daily in crowds to die on the scaffold, a certain man saved a prisoner in this way. The prisoner and his friend were much alike in size and appearance. Just before the fatal day of execution, this friend visited the prisoner, and contrived to exchange clothes with him, and to remain in the prison, whilst the condemned man went out free. And then in a few hours the end came, and the friend died for him he loved. Many long years ago, in the old days, a great battle took place in Scotland, between two clans who were enemies. The fierce warriors of those times honoured and loved their chief above all men, and were ready to die for him. So in this battle of which I speak, the sons of one man were appointed to stand round the chief and protect him. The old man loved his tall, brave sons dearly, but he did not hesitate to give their lives for that of his chief. And so as each of his sons fell mortally wounded, he cried out, " Another for Hector," and instantly another son sprang to his chieftain's side to fight and die like the last. And at last, when all his sons had fallen, the old man himself fought by his chief and fell. Perhaps some of you have heard what a brave Swiss did long ago in a battle against the Austrians. The Swiss soldiers fought manfully, but the Austrians were too strong for them, and they formed a line with their spears fixed, which the Swiss tried in vain to break through. At length one man, a simple countryman in the ranks of the Swiss, said, " Take care of my wife and children, I will break through their line." So saying he rushed upon the line of spears, receiving them in his breast and arms, and though he fell dead, pierced by many wounds, the line was for a moment broken, and the

Swiss rushed through the fence which his death had
opened. But, dear children, what are these things com-
pared to the death of Jesus, our Friend? He died for
all men, not for His friends, but for His enemies. God
became man, and suffered death for those whom He
had created. And this Friend of little children is an
unchanging friend. We know that

> " Our earthly friends may fail us,
> And change with changing years ;"

Many of your schoolmates whom you call friends now,
will forget you when they go out into the world. But
Jesus is a Friend who never forgets us, however much
we may neglect Him.

Next, the Hymn tells us that—

> " There's a rest for little children
> Above the bright blue sky,
> Who love the Blessèd Saviour,
> And to the Father cry ;
> A rest from every turmoil,
> From sin and sorrow free,
> Where every little pilgrim
> Shall rest eternally."

Ah! dear little ones, you all know what a blessed
thing rest is. You know what it is to come home after
a long day in school, or after a long ramble in the lanes
and woods, looking forward to sleep and rest. And as
you grow older and go out into the world, and journey

on till your day's work be done, you will often be very, very weary, and long for rest. There will be rough roads for you little pilgrims to walk on, and steep hills of difficulty to climb, and sharp thorns of sorrow to tear and wound. But still for God's children there is a promised rest; rest here in earth, but often disturbed and broken; rest in Heaven hereafter, perfect and eternal. I do not mean that you will be idle in Heaven. That would not be happiness. But there you will have rest from sin, rest from temptation, rest from pain and sorrow, and

> " Every little pilgrim
> Shall rest eternally."

And next, the Hymn tells us that—

> " There's a home for little children
> Above the bright blue sky,
> Where Jesus reigns in glory,
> A home of peace and joy;
> No home on earth is like it,
> Nor can with it compare;
> For every one is happy,
> Nor could be happier there."

You all love your home, my children, it is the sweetest, dearest word we have. And one of the hardest things which we have to do is to leave home for the first time, and go forth among strangers. But our home on earth is not always what we would wish it to be. There are often angry tempers and cruel words there, which make home miserable. Sickness, and want, and trouble often come and make home very dark and wretched. Sometimes our home is broken up, the old house has to be left; the place where we played as children will never know us again. Well, then, we must remember that God's children have a home

   " Above the bright blue sky,"

where no trouble or strife can ever enter,

   " For every one is happy,
   Nor could be happier there."

And what do you think makes this home better than any other? Because Jesus is there. We know that Jesus is with us in our earthly homes, if only we are trying to be good. A little child was once asked where Jesus was, and he answered, " He lives in our street now." And the child was right, for " where two or three are gathered together in His Name, there is He in the midst of them." But here we can only see Jesus by faith, but in that home above we shall see Him face to face.

  Next, the Hymn goes on to tell us that—

   " There's a crown for little children
   Above the bright blue sky,
   And all who look for Jesus,
   Shall wear it by and by;
   A crown of brightest glory,
   Which He will then bestow,
   On those who found His favour,
   And loved His Name below."

Now tell me, my children, who are those who wear a crown? Kings and queens, you answer. Yes, but there are others who were crowned in former times. When men ran races amongst the old Greeks and Romans, the winner received a crown, which was made of parsley, or some other plant. This crown was highly prized as the mark of victory, but on the day after the race it was withered and worthless. S. Paul was thinking of this when he said, " they do it to obtain a corruptible crown, but we an incorruptible." You all have a race to run, my children, the race of holiness, the race along the narrow way from earth to Heaven; and do you know how you must run this race? " With patience, looking unto Jesus." But there were others who were crowned in old times, the conquerors who had gained a victory. Now we have a battle to fight, a very hard battle indeed. We have to fight against sin, against temptation, against bad temper, against ourselves. And if by God's help we conquer, we shall receive a crown which never fades. Once there was a little boy who used to go every morning to the Church very early, to assist the Priest in the service. It was winter time and bitterly cold. The roads were white with snow, and the frost was thick upon tree and window. One morning the little server-boy went to Church, and lighted the candles, and prepared for the Priest, but the old man did not come. He lay warm in bed, and thought no one will be at Church this bitter morning, why should I go? The next day came, and the cold was even more severe. The little boy lying warm in bed thought, why should I go forth and face the snow and ice? The Priest will not be there. Then he remembered it was his duty, so he went forth as before to the Church, but the old Priest was again absent. The third morning dawned dark and cold as ever; and again the little boy was tempted to neglect his duty, but he struggled with the temptation, and went as before to Church. Meanwhile, as the aged Priest lay in his bed, he saw a vision or dream, in which he beheld the Lord coming to him with three crowns in His hand. The old man stretched forth his hands, eagerly crying, "Are these for me, my Master?" And the Lord answered, "Not for thee, but for the little server-boy. Thrice he has been tempted, thrice he has resisted. Crowns are for those who conquer, not for those who fail." Dear children, "hold that fast which thou hast, that no man take thy crown."

And again, the Hymn tells us that—

> " There's a song for little children
> Above the bright blue sky,
> A song that will not weary,
> Though sung continually;
> A song which even angels;
> Can never, never sing;
> They know not Christ as Saviour,
> But worship Him as King."

All little children love singing, and I know in my own parish I hear the children on their way to school, and the young lads ploughing in the fields, singing our bright Church hymns oftener than other songs. But you know, children, that all have not an ear for music; there are some boys who could not sing correctly however hard they might try. And we know too that we can only sing "the Lord's Song" here on earth for a little while. Death comes and hushes the music here for ever. But we know this also, which is the best thing of all to know, that if we have praised God here, "not only with our lips, but in our lives," we shall one day take part in the perfect song "Above the bright sky." And that song which we shall sing in Heaven is even better than any which the holy angels sing. Very often we hear people say, "I want to be an angel, and with the angels dwell;" and sometimes parents speaking of a dead child say, " my darling is an angel in Heaven." But when we die we do not become angels. They are a different order of beings, created by God before man was created, for we know that "man was made a little lower than the angels." If we are permitted to enter Heaven we shall be able to sing what the angels cannot sing, the story of the Cross, the praise of the Precious Blood which redeemed us from our sins.

> " Alleluia we sing in the Church we love,
> Alleluia resounds in the Church above ;

To Thy little ones, Lord, may such grace be given,
That we lose not our part in the song of Heaven."

And once more, the Hymn tells us that—

" There's a robe for little children
Above the bright blue sky,
And a harp of sweetest music,
And palms of victory."

And for whom is that white robe prepared? For God's
saints, no matter whether they be little children, or old
men and women. For all whose sins are forgiven them,
through the precious Blood of Christ, and who try to lead
good lives by God's help. For you, dear little children,
are the Friend, and the rest, and the home, and the
crown, and the song, and the pure white robe; try then
to live as God's children here in earth, that you may one
day have the Children's Portion in Heaven. Ask the
Friend of little children to be your Friend, and let your
prayer be now—

" Lord, grant Thy little children
To know Thee as their own."

N

" We are but little children weak,
Not born to any high estate ;
What can we do for Jesus' sake
Who is so high and good and great ?

" We know the Holy Innocents
Laid down for Him their infant life,
And Martyrs brave and patient saints
Have stood for Him in fire and strife.

" We wear the cross they wore of old,
Our lips have learned like vows to make ;
We need not die ; we cannot fight ;
What may we do for Jesus' sake.

" Oh, day by day, each Christian child
Has much to do, without, within ;
A death to die for Jesus' sake,
A weary war to wage with sin.

" When deep within our swelling hearts
The thoughts of pride and anger rise,
When bitter words are on our tongues,
And tears of passion in our eyes ;

" Then we may stay the angry blow,
Then we may check the hasty word,
Give gentle answers back again,
And fight a battle for the Lord.

" With smiles of peace, and looks of love,
Light in our dwellings we may make,
Bid kind good humour brighten there,
And still do all for Jesus' sake.

" There's not a child so small and weak
But has his little cross to take,
His little work of love and praise
That he may do for Jesus' sake."

SERMON XXII.

Little Lives.

(FOR A CHILDREN'S SERVICE.)

PROVERBS XX. 11.

" *Even a child is known by his doings.*"

THE Hymn which we have just sung tells us what " little children weak" can do for Jesus Christ. Just as there is no insect too tiny, no leaf, or speck of dust in the universe too small to have its place and its work in God's great workshop, so there is no child too small or weak to have a place in God's Church. Do not think, my children, that when you grow up to be men and women you will do some great work for God. Everything in nature begins from a small commencement; so you must begin as little children with little feet to tread in the path of duty, and with little hands to do little acts for Christ's dear sake.

> " We know the holy Innocents
> Laid down for Him their infant life ;
> And martyr's brave, and patient saints,
> Have stood for Him in fire and strife,
> We wear the Cross they wore of old,
> Our lips have learned like vows to make ;
> We need not die; we cannot fight ;
> What may we do for Jesus' sake ?"

No, dear children, you are not called upon to die for Jesus, but to *live* for Him, and that is sometimes the harder task of the two. Your little lives may be, and ought to be, beautiful with the beauty of holiness. I want specially to talk to you now about your influence over your companions, and about little efforts to do good. Do not think—I am too small to do anything. You know the great oak trees which grow in our parish, so large that twenty little children can shelter underneath one of them. Well, how did those giant trees begin?—from a tiny acorn. Have you ever seen an engine-driver pouring oil on the machinery of his engine? It seems a very little thing which he is doing, only dropping a few drops of oil here and there; and yet without that oil the machinery would not work. I dare say you have seen men building a church or a house. At first you saw only one brick or stone placed upon another, and it seemed as though the work would never be done, yet the house grew and was finished. Thus, Rome and London started from one brick. Some of the greatest discoveries have started from small beginnings. Sir Isaac Newton was sitting in his garden when the sight of an apple falling from a tree suggested the theory of gravitation. James Watt was looking at a tea-kettle when the first thought of the steam engine came to him. These small beginnings were followed out with patience, and ended in great scientific triumphs, according to the Eastern proverb, which says, that "Time and patience change the mulberry leaf to satin."

> "Think naught a trifle, though it small appear ;
> Small sands the mountains, moments make the year,
> And trifles, life."

Now, each of you little children can do something for Jesus Christ : it was for this purpose that you were sent into the world. One thing you cannot help doing, and that is to *influence* your companions, to lead them right or wrong, just according as you do right or wrong yourselves. Perhaps you think—I am only one, what influence or power have I got over others ? But remember it is the one individual, not the crowd, who influences others. "All the great things have been done by *the ones*," as a writer says very truly. It required *one* Samson to deliver Israel, and *one* David to kill Goliath, and *one* Wellington to win Waterloo.

So one good child in a school may do a vast amount of good, and one bad child can poison the lives of hundreds, just as a few drops of bad water leaking into a well may destroy a whole parish. A chemist will tell you that one grain of the drug called iodine will colour seven thousand times its weight of water. So the influence of a little child will give a colour to a whole school or parish. And so the influence of *one* bad habit, or *one* bad book, will change a whole life and character. They say that if a single seed of the Canada thistle, hidden away among the straw of a packing case, happens to drop on congenial soil, it will soon increase so as to spoil acres of ground. So, little children, the little acts and words of your little lives are able to do a great deal of good or harm. The little acts and duties of everyday life are the most important of all.

> " Oh, day by day, each Christian child
> Has much to do, without, within;
> A death to die for Jesus' sake,
> A weary war to wage with sin.

> " With smiles of peace, and looks of love,
> Light in our dwellings we may make,
> Bid kind good humour brighten there,
> And still do all for Jesus' sake."

It is not the great torrent, like Niagara, but the little trickling stream which makes the meadows fertile. And so it is not so much the great work of the hero or the martyr which makes up a Christian life, as the quiet virtues of everyday life ; such virtues as gentleness, meekness, patience and forbearance. These are virtues which God's children should display, and by them little lives are made divine. Every effort which you make to do right, although it may be only a little one, God sees and accepts. When things vex you in school, or at home, and you feel inclined to get into a passion, and to say angry words, and when you struggle against that temptation, and conquer it, then you have fought a battle

for the Lord, and the Lord will not forget it. You have
fought for your colours, the banner of the Cross. At the
battle of Albuera, the French had almost cut one of our
regiments to pieces. A desperate fight took place for the
colours. The ensign who carried the flag was cut down,
and the colours seized by the enemy, but after a struggle
over his dead body the flag was once more recovered.
The second ensign was severely wounded, but he tore
the tattered colours from the flag-staff, and placed them
in his breast, where they were found after the battle,
soaked with his blood. That is how brave men fought
for the flag of their regiment. You, dear children, have
a harder and a nobler battle still to fight, since to conquer *ourselves* is the grandest of all victories.

> " When deep within our swelling hearts
> The thoughts of pride and anger rise,
> When bitter words are on our tongues,
> And tears of passion in our eyes ;
>
> " Then we may stay the angry blow,
> Then we may check the hasty word,
> Give gentle answers back again,
> And fight a battle for the Lord."

There is a beautiful legend of the olden days which
tells us how a young man found a blue forget-me-not,
one of a kind which blooms but once in seven years.
He who carries it in his breast can surmount all difficulties,

and discover all secrets and hidden treasures. So the
young man of the legend placed the flower in his breast,
and set forth on his journey. No bolts or bars could
check him on his way, no hill however steep, could hinder his journey. At length, as he climbed higher and
higher up a mountain, he came to a rock which barred
his farther progress. No sooner did he press against it
with his breast, where lay the flower, than the rock
opened, and he beheld within vast treasures of gold and
silver, and precious stones. Eagerly stooping to gather
up the glittering wealth around him, he loaded himself
with treasures; but as he stooped to seize yet more, the
flower dropped unheeded from his breast. Turning to
leave the cavern with his treasure, he fancied he heard a
faint voice whisper, "Forget me not! forget me not!"
but his very ears were filled with precious jewels, and he
heeded not; and presently the rocks around him fell, and
overwhelmed him. Now, dear children, I can see a
parable in that old legend. Jesus has given each of you,
His children, a flower to wear; that flower is *Holiness*,
and you are bidden to go forth on life's journey—
" Wearing the white flower of a blameless life." That
flower will help you to climb above all difficulties, and it
will open to you such treasures as the world does not
dream of, the treasures of God's love. But take heed
lest you lose your flower. Take heed, lest while you are
seeking the world's treasure, and are busy with your

work, or your play, you lose the white flower of Holiness, of Purity,—

"A little flower, that ne'er again,
Though sought in penitence and pain,
Once lost, thou ever canst regain—
Forget it not! Forget it not!"

THE END.

www.ingramcontent.com/pod-product-compliance
Lightning Source LLC
Chambersburg PA
CBHW030826270326
41928CB00007B/914